Communication Vibrations

Larry L. Barker

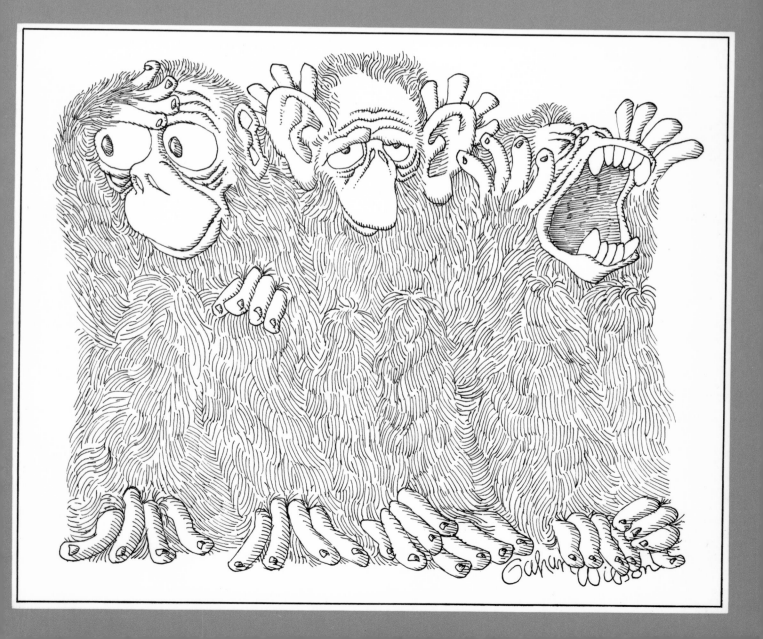

Communication
Vibrations

Communication Vibrations

Larry Lee Barker

Florida State University

Prentice-Hall, Inc., Englewood Cliffs, New Jersey

Library of Congress Cataloging in Publication Data

Barker, Larry Lee, 1941-   comp.
    Communication vibrations.

    (Prentice-Hall series in speech communication)
    Includes bibliograhpical references.
    1. Communication.   I. Title.
P90.B298   001.5   73-19516
ISBN 0-13-153007-0

PRENTICE-HALL SERIES IN SPEECH COMMUNICATION
Larry L. Barker and Robert Kibler, editors

Printed in the United States of America

10   9   8   7   6   5   4   3   2   1

Credits for text and pictures are listed on page 143.

Prentice-Hall International, Inc., London
Prentice-Hall of Australia, Pty., Sydney
Prentice-Hall of Canada, Ltd., Toronto
Prentice-Hall of India Private Limited, New Delhi
Prentice-Hall of Japan, Inc., Tokyo

contents

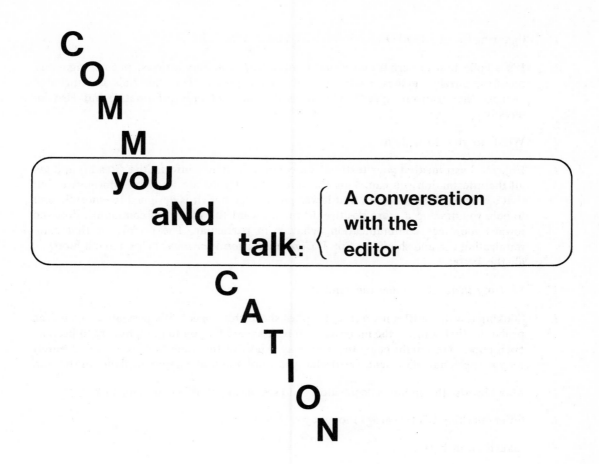

COMMUNICATION

yoU aNd I talk: { A conversation with the editor

SETTING: Any college campus
PARTICIPANTS: U (student) and I (editor)
TIME: Now

After picking up a copy of Communication Vibrations, *U opens it, turns to this page and speaks:*

U: Just out of curiosity, what is a communication vibration?

I: A communication vibration is a gut feeling. It is something you feel about your own or someone else's verbal or nonverbal messages. It defies logical or systematic definition, yet many people stake small fortunes on the basis of it. A communication vibration is an attitude that you bring into a communication setting; it is a humanistic emotion that you rely on intuitively. In short, a communication vibration is how you feel about communication and communicating.

U: How can a book be a communication vibration?

I: It can't. That's why this is not a book. Books dealing with communication often send "bad" vibrations to students. They smack of routine learning, statistical studies, and all of the traditional things that are necessary but not very interesting. Books, of course, are useful in informing students about principles and research, but they usually do little to excite them about the communication process. And, if you aren't excited about something, will you *really* learn it?

U: (ignoring the question) OK, so if this isn't a book, what is it?

I: It's a collection of verbal and visual materials. It contains articles, poems, vignettes, pictures, puzzles, games, cartoons, and even a poster. The materials are included because they transmit specific vibrations that are not only informative but also interesting.

U: What do you do with it?

I: Enjoy it. I assume that your textbook on communication is informative. Read it and get all the information you can. This collection of materials also may be informative, but that's only part of the reason that it was pulled together. It is designed to entertain and to help you develop a more positive attitude toward the subject of communication and toward your own communication behavior in particular. The premise is that communication can and should be fun. If *Communication Vibrations* helps make it more so, all the better.

U: Will my instructor make me read it?

I: (looking down, shuffles his feet and replies sheepishly) I guess it's possible, maybe even probable, that some of the materials will be assigned for you to read, but try to keep an open mind. You might enjoy them anyway. Many of the materials are included purely for your personal enjoyment. Read what you want and make paper airplanes of the rest.

U: May I browse through this "collection" and see for myself if I want to read it?

I: (after checking U's ID card) I thought you'd never ask!

U   take it from here. . . .

Communication
Vibrations

Since communication is the glue
that holds individuals together in society,
I cannot help but wonder
whether society would run better
if communication worked better. And when I
wonder how to improve communication,
I realize that most of our failures
in understanding one another
have less to do with what is said and
heard than with what is intended
and what is inferred.
As my own small gift toward a
peaceful world, therefore, I would
like to be able to offer some way,
some addition to our present
channels of interaction, that would
communicate our intentions
as clearly and as accurately as words
now communicate our ideas.
I cannot really foresee what it
would be like to live in a world
without deceit, but I cannot imagine
it would be any worse.

George A. Miller
President, American Psychological Association

How Words Change Our Lives

S. I. Hayakawa

Hayakawa is one of the best-known advocates of a discipline called "general semantics." In this piece, he defines general semantics and illustrates the relationships among words, meaning, and human behavior.

The end product of education, yours and mine and everybody's, is the total pattern of reactions and possible reactions we have inside ourselves. If you did not have within you at this moment the pattern of reactions which we call "the ability to read English," you would see here only meaningless black marks on paper. Because of the trained patterns of response, you are (or are not) stirred to patriotism by martial music, your feelings of reverence are aroused by the symbols of your religion, you listen more respectfully to the health advice of someone who has "M.D." after his name than to that of someone who hasn't. What I call here a "pattern of reactions," then, is the sum total of the ways we act in response to events, to words and to symbols.

Our reaction patterns — our semantic habits, as we may call them — are the internal and most important residue of whatever years of education or miseducation we may have received from our parents' conduct toward us in childhood as well as their teachings, from the formal education we may have had, from all the sermons and lectures we have listened to, from the radio programs and the movies and television shows we have experienced, from all the books and newspapers and comic strips we have read, from the conversations we have had with friends and associates, and from all our experiences. If, as the result of all these influences that make us what we are, our semantic habits are reasonably similar to those of most people around us, we are regarded as "well-adjusted," or "normal," and perhaps "dull." If our semantic habits are noticeably different from those of others, we are regarded as "individual-istic" or "original," or, if the differences are disapproved of or viewed with alarm, as "screwball" or "crazy."

Semantics is sometimes defined in dictionaries as "the science of the meaning of words" — which would not be a bad definition if people didn't assume that the search for the meanings of words begins and ends with looking them up in a dictionary.

If one stops to think for a moment, it is clear that to define a word, as a dictionary does, is simply to explain the word with more words. To be thorough about defining, we should next have to define the words used in the definition, then define the words used in defining the words used in the definition . . . and so on. Defining words with more words, in short, gets us at once into what mathematics call an "infinite regress." Alternatively, it can get us into the kind of runaround we sometimes encounter when we look up "impertinence" and find it defined as "impudence," so we look up "impudence" and find it defined as "impertinence." Yet — and here we come to another common reaction pattern — people often act as if words can be explained fully with more words. To a person who asked for a definition of jazz, Louis Armstrong is said to have replied, "Man, when you got to ask what it is, you'll never get to know," proving himself to be an intuitive semanticist as well as a great trumpet player. . . .

A basic idea in general semantics, therefore, is that the meaning of words (or other symbols) is not in the words, but in our own semantic reactions. If I were to tell a shocking obscene story in Arabic or Hindustani or Swahili before an audience that understood only English, no one would blush or be angry; the story would be neither shocking nor obscene — indeed, it would not even be a story. Likewise, the value of a dollar bill is not in the bill, but in our social agreement to accept it as a symbol of value. If that agreement were to break down through the collapse of our Government, the dollar bill would become only a scrap of paper. We do not understand a dollar bill by staring at it long and hard. We understand it by observing how people act with respect to it. We understand it by understanding the social mechanisms and the loyalties that keep it meaningful. Semantics is therefore a social study, basic to all other social studies.

It is often remarked that words are tricky — and that we are all prone to be deceived by "fast talkers," such as high-pressure salesmen, skillful propagandists, politicians or lawyers. Since few of us are aware of the degree to which we use words to deceive ourselves, the sin of "using words in a tricky way" is one that is always attributed to the other fellow. When the Russians use the word "democracy" to mean something quite different from what we mean by it, we at once accuse them of "propaganda," of "corrupting the meanings of words." But when we use the word "democracy" in the United States to mean something quite different from what the Russians mean by it, they are equally quick to accuse us of "hypocrisy." We all tend to believe that the way we use words is the correct way, and that people who use the same words in other ways are either ignorant or dishonest.

Leaving aside for a moment such abstract and difficult terms as "democracy," let us examine a common, everyday word like "frog." Surely there is no problem about what "frog" means! Here are some sample sentences:

"If we're going fishing, we'll have to catch some frogs first." (This is easy.)

"I have a frog in my throat." (You can hear it croaking.)

"She wore a loose, silk jacket fastened with braided frogs."

"The blacksmith pared down the frog and the hoof before shoeing the horse."

"In Hamilton, Ohio, there is a firm by the name of American Frog and Switch Company."

In addition to these "frogs," there is the frog in which a sword is carried, the frog at the bottom of a bowl or vase that is used in flower arrangement, and the frog which is part of a violin bow. The reader can no doubt think of other "frogs."

Or take another common word such as "order." There is the *order* that the salesman tries to get, which is

quite different from the *order* which a captain gives to his crew. Some people enter holy *orders*. There is the *order* in the house when mother has finished tidying up; there is the batting *order* of the home team; there is an *order* of ham and eggs. It is surprising that with so many meanings to the word, people don't misunderstand one another oftener than they do.

The foregoing are only striking examples of a principle to which we are all so well accustomed that we rarely think of it; namely, that most words have more meanings than dictionaries can keep track of. And when we consider further that each of us has different experiences, different memories, different likes and dislikes, it is clear that all words evoke different responses in all of us. We may agree as to what the term "Mississippi River" stands for, but you and I recall different parts of the river; you and I have had different experiences with it; one of us has read more about it than the other; one of us may have happy memories of it, while the other may recall chiefly tragic events connected with it. Hence your "Mississippi River" can never be identical with my "Mississippi River." The fact that we can communicate with each other about the "Mississippi River" often conceals the fact that we are talking about two different sets of memories and experiences.

Words being as varied in their meaning as they are, no one can tell us what the correct interpretation of a word should be in advance of our next encounter with that word. The reader may have been taught always to revere the word "mother." But what is he going to do the next time he encounters this word, when it occurs in the sentence "Mother began to form in the bottle"? If it is impossible to determine what a single word will mean on next encounter, is it possible to say in advance what is the correct evaluation of such events as these: (1) next summer, an individual who calls himself a socialist will announce his candidacy for the office of register of deeds in your city; (2) next autumn, there will be a strike at one of your local department stores; (3) next week, your wife will announce that she is going to change her style of hairdo; (4) tomorrow, your little boy will come home with a bleeding nose?

A reasonably sane individual will react to each of these events in his own way, according to time, place and the entire surrounding set of circumstances; and included among those circumstances will be his own stock of experiences, wishes, hopes and fears. But there are people whose pattern of reactions is such that some of them can be completely predicted in advance. Mr. A will never vote for anyone called "socialist," no matter how incompetent or crooked the alternative candidates

3

may be. Mr. B-1 always disapproves of strikes and strikers, without bothering to inquire whether or not this strike has its justifications; Mr. B-2 always sympathizes with the strikers because he hates all bosses. Mr. C belongs to the "stay sweet as you are" school of thought, so that his wife hasn't been able to change her hairdo since she left high school. Mr. D always faints at the sight of blood.

Such fixed and unalterable patterns of reaction — in their more obvious forms we call them prejudices — are almost inevitably organized around words. Mr. E distrusts and fears all people to whom the term "Catholic" is applicable, while Mr. F, who is Catholic, distrusts and fears all non-Catholics. Mr. G is so rabid a Republican that he reacts with equal dislike to all Democrats, all Democratic proposals, all opposite proposals if they are also made by Democrats. Back in the days when Franklin D. Roosevelt was President, Mr. G disliked not only the Democratic President but also his wife, children and dog. His office was on Roosevelt Road in Chicago (it had been named after Theodore Roosevelt), but he had his address changed to his back door on 11th Street, so that he would not have to print the hated name on his stationery. Mr. H, on the other hand, is an equally rabid Democrat, who hates himself for continuing to play golf, since golf is Mr. Eisenhower's favorite game. People suffering from such prejudices seem to have in their brains an uninsulated spot which, when touched by such words as "capitalist," "boss," "striker," "scab," "Democrat," "Republican," "socialized medicine," and other such loaded terms, results in an immediate short circuit, often with a blowing of fuses.

Alfred Korzybski, the founder of general semantics, called such short-circuited responses "identification reactions." He used the word "identification" in a special sense; he meant that persons given to such fixed patterns of response identify (that is, treat as identical) all occurrences of a given word or symbol; they identify all the different cases that fall under the same name. Thus, if one has hostile identification reactions to "women drivers," then all women who drive cars are "identical" in their incompetence. . . .

Our everyday habits of speech and our unconscious assumptions about the relations between words and things lead, then, to an identification reaction in which it is felt that all things that have the same name are entitled to the same response. From this point of view, all "insurance men," or "college boys," or "politicians," or "lawyers," or "Texans" are alike. Once we recognize the absurdity of these identification reactions based on identities of name, we can begin to think more clearly and more adequately. No "Texan" is exactly like any other "Texan." No "college boy" is exactly like any other "college boy." Most of the time "Texans" or "college boys" may be what you think they are: but often they are not. To realize fully the difference between words and what they stand for is to be ready for differences as well as similarities in the world. This readiness is mandatory to scientific thinking, as well as to sane thinking.

Korzybski's simple but powerful suggestion to those wishing to improve their semantic habits is to add "index numbers" to all terms, according to the formula: A_1 is not A_2. Translated into everyday language we can state the formula in such terms as these. Cow_1 is not cow_2; cow_2 is not cow_3; $Texan_1$ is not $Texan_2$; politician$_1$ is not politician$_2$; ham and eggs (Plaza Hotel) are not ham and eggs (Smitty's Cafe); socialism (Russia) is not socialism (England); private enterprise (Joe's Shoe Repair Shop) is not private enterprise (A.T.&T.). The formula means that instead of simply thinking about "cows" or "politicians" or "private enterprise," we should think as factually as possible about the differences between one cow and another, one politician and another, one privately owned enterprise and another.

This device of "indexing" will not automatically make us wiser and better, but it's a start. When we talk or write, the habit of indexing our general terms will reduce our tendency to wild and woolly generalization. It will compel us to think before we speak — think in terms of concrete objects and events and situations, rather than in terms of verbal associations. When we read or listen, the habit of indexing will help us visualize more concretely, and therefore understand better, what is being said. And if nothing is being said except deceptive windbaggery, the habit of indexing may — at least part of the time — save us from snapping, like the pickerel, at phony minnows. Another way of summing up is to remember, as Wendell Johnson said, that "To a mouse, cheese is cheese — that's why mousetraps work."

4

MEANING?

Again I find that
My words do not mean
The same thing
In your ear and
My mind.
The problem we spoke of
Remains
Clamped by obscurities
Like a fishhook
Snagged on weeds.
We should have used
A net.
But that would have
Required
Synchronized exertion and
Willingness
To share the catch.

Virginia Bailey

This brief article suggests that we are often underwhelmed by overuse of "Hot Language"!

HOT LANGUAGE AND COOL LIVES

Arthur Berger

There is a fish that always delights me whenever I take my children to the aquarium. It is a slender rather trivial thing that has the ability to puff itself up into a big ball and scare off (hopefully) other fish that might wish to attack it. It is literally a big windbag, yet this defense mechanism works—well enough, at least, for other windbags to be born and survive.

The whole business is quite absurd except that it does work, and what is more fantastic, with people as well as with fishes. A lot of people are leading rather luke-warm lives, if not cool (and not in the sense of "good" as some use the term) or tepid lives, yet they describe themselves and their actions in terms of what might be called "hot" language.

5

I can recall once overhearing two bored youths at a tennis court. Said one of them, "Let's split," a phrase much in usage these days, in fitting with the schizophrenic nature of the times. Somehow "splitting" from a place is much more exciting than "going someplace else" or "leaving."

Is it not possible that there is a direct correlation between a growing sense of powerlessness and futility in our lives and the jazzed-up language we use? The more you feel yourself diminished the more you "build yourself up" by using hot language, showing that you are in some kind of an "in" group, and know what's going on. It is only natural to try to represent oneself in the best possible light, but if we study the way people do this, we find that this hot or inflated language is somewhat self-defeating.

As everything becomes inflated and *tremendous,* the word loses its currency. What is normal becomes tremendous. What then do we say about something that really is tremendous? It seems that the more we use hot language to add color to our otherwise colorless lives, the less utility the hot language has; it becomes devalued, and we have to work harder for less, so to speak. What used to be large is now "Giant king size," and we have reached the point of no return.

Perhaps there is some kind of a searching for the infinite at work. In a recent advertisement from a humane society, various kinds of memberships were announced: Annual $5, Patron $10, Life $100, Perpetual $250. A lifetime is no longer enough. We must have a rate for those who would be immortal. On the opposite side of the fence death must be made more final, somehow. Thus we find ads for insecticides claiming that they "kill bugs *dead!*"

It may be that we can now think of killing without death—for as everything grows out of control and the fantastic becomes the commonplace (men on the moon on prime-time television), the old words like the old lifestyle become, somehow, inadequate. We need more and more emphasis and must be told that when something is killed it will be dead.

Television commercials have bred within the average American a skepticism that must somehow be overcome. We find all about us claims that are obviously absurd: on menus, travel brochures, book-jackets, etc. The law of diminishing returns is at work. Since people now believe less and less, you have to promise more and more to come out even. In this sense advertising is self-defeating for it (more than anything else) has created this skepticism, which it keeps attacking and reinforcing at the same time.

The use of this hot language is symptomatic of a certain malaise affecting people, which leads them to believe that life must at all times be exciting, vital, dazzling, full of "fabulous" experiences. This is nonsense, obviously. Everyone—even "world historical figures" such as leaders of great nations or movie celebrities—spends a great deal of his time doing routine, ordinary things. Thus, the use of hot language makes us *devalue* our lives, since we take a rather absurd conception of what is normal, measure our lives against this false norm, and find ourselves wanting. We all want to lead Giant King Size lives in an age when there are few giants or kings. Since we cannot, we then define ourselves as leading lives of quiet desperation, describe life as absurd and meaningless, and try to escape from all this by consumerism, drugs, or some other kind of narcoticism.

A distinguished sociologist, Leo Lowenthal, has discussed a form of hot language, the use of "superlatives," in the following manner:

> This wholesale distribution of highest ratings defeats its own purpose. Everything is presented as something unique, unheard of, outstanding. Thus nothing is unique, unheard of, outstanding. Totality of the superlative means totality of the mediocre. It levels the presentation of human life to the presentation of merchandise.

He wrote this in reference to the tendency of contemporary writers to use superlatives in biographies done for popular magazines. Lowenthal noticed that there was a change from early biographies that didn't use superlatives and dealt with heroes of production to recent biographies (around 1940) that used superlatives and were about heroes of consumption. On first sight the superlatives didn't seem very significant, until their real function was discovered. This was, Lowenthal suggested, to create "a reign of psychic terror, where the masses have to realize the pettiness and insignificance of their everyday life. The already weakened consciousness of being an individual is struck another heavy blow by the pseudo-individualizing forces of the superlative."

This was written in the forties, when we had "stars." How does the ordinary man feel in the seventies in an era when being a "star" is no longer significant, since we now have "*superstars.*" When the star is relegated to mediocrity, what do we say about the average citizen? The fact is significant that we now use terms such as the "little guy"; his stature and significance is diminishing greatly, and he is on the verge of becoming a "forgotten" American.

Even so the tongue is a little member, and boasteth great things. Behold, how great a matter a little fire kindleth!

And the tongue is a fire, a world of iniquity: so is the tongue among our members, that it defileth the whole body, and setteth on fire the course of nature; and it is set on fire of hell.

But the tongue can no man tame; it is an unruly evil, full of deadly poison.

Therewith bless we God, even the Father; and therewith curse we men, which are made after the similitude of God.

Out of the same mouth proceedeth blessing and cursing. My brethren, these things ought not so to be.

Doth a fountain send forth at the same place sweet water and bitter?

James 3:5-6, 8-11

PATTERNS

OF SPEECH

ARTIST: BOB CLARKE
IDEA BY MAX BRANDEL

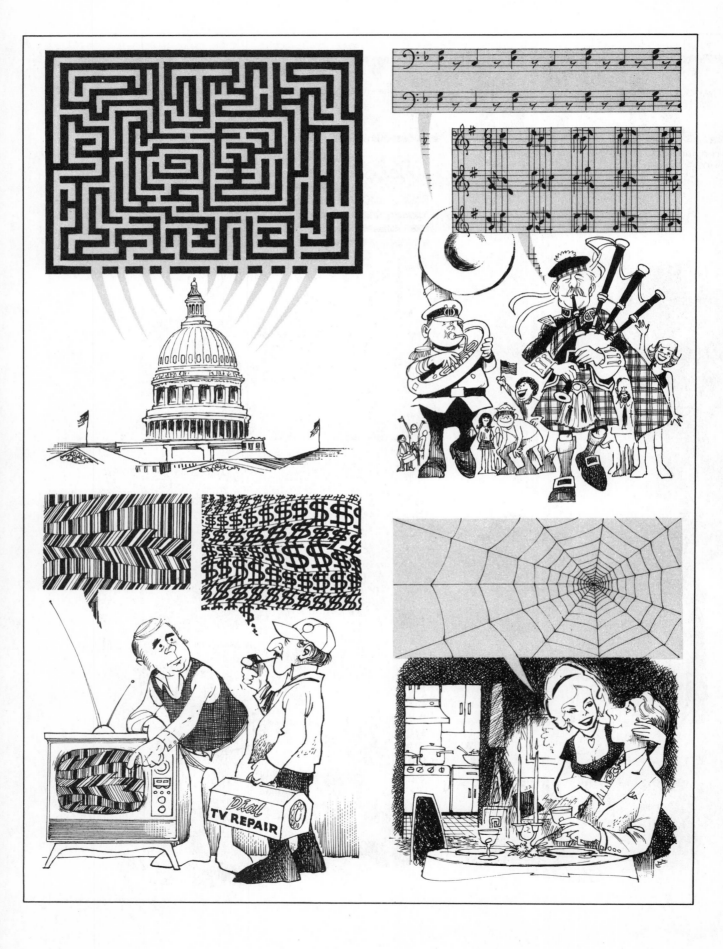

This game was created especially for this volume. Not only will you enjoy playing it with friends, but you should learn something about yourself at the same time.

MIRROR / RORRIM

Loretta Malandro

"YOU DON'T LOOK LIKE THE TYPE" SYNDROME

Human beings continually make assumptions and inferences about other people based on a number of verbal and nonverbal cues. In meeting a person we often allow ourselves to make quick generalizations concerning his profession, interests, temperament, abilities, and sexual activities along with a number of other assumptions.

First impressions, regardless of their validity, often play a significant role in our relation to others. It is not uncommon to hear an employer, after an interview with a prospective salesman, comment, "Bill just doesn't look like the aggressive type." Larry, in deciding whether to ask Barb or Lori to go horseback riding, asks Lori because "Barb just doesn't look like the outdoors type."

An individual has a number of different self-types—one for home, one for work, one for friends, and so forth. These self-types can tend to be rather constraining unless we understand them and, hopefully, learn how to control them.

THE MISUNDERSTANDING ABOUT MISPERCEPTION

Barb, sitting with her legs crossed, her arms tightly folded over her chest, tapping her foot impatiently, scowls at Jim when he enters the room. Jim, deciding that this is not the time to "hang around," makes his visit very brief. Barb, in a state of shock, cannot understand what made Jim rush off! These types of situations are often accompanied with such statements as "I don't understand what gave him that impression!" These statements simply illustrate that we often have very little control over our projected self-types.

An earlier version of this game was designed by Loretta Malandro, Robert Spell, and Arlie Parks, Florida State University, Summer 1972

Understanding our self-types is a prerequisite to controlling and directing the things we call "images." Often, easily identifiable items, such as clothing and hairstyle, including more abstract concepts such as the "air about the person"—will contribute to others' impressions of us. Sometimes we hear senseless statements such as "I don't think Steve is shy at all—we must not be talking about the same person." In one sense this statement is quite accurate, for we are different people in different situations. It becomes a senseless statement when we deny the fact that these different "persons" or "self-types" exist. Given this perspective, the question "who am I" should be "who are we," and "self-concept" should be "concept of selves."

The next time you start to tell another person that they have "misperceived" you—stop and think. Perhaps you have just misprojected your self-type!

MIRROR, MIRROR ON THE WALL

The game "Mirror/rorriM" is designed to provide a reflection of how others perceive you in a given situation. Each player "types" other players by selecting a picture in various categories. The categories range from abstract concepts, such as color and seasonings and spices, to more concrete areas, such as sex and after-marriage. With both types of categories it is important to keep in mind that the "meanings are in the people" and not in the pictures.

The most revealing part of the game occurs in the discussions following the selection of "types" for each player. These discussions usually provide important information concerning the reasons that other players made certain assumptions about you. Often these reasons are more important than the assumptions themselves!

When the Queen asked the mirror who was the "fairest of them all," she became quite dissatisfied when it told her that Snow White was the fairest. You may be dissatisfied with others' perceptions of you, but don't make the mistake that the Queen made by trying to banish Snow White from her kingdom. The problems and the answers related to your self-types are within you! "Mirror/rorriM" is just a starting point to help you in understanding and eventually controlling and directing your self-types.

COOKBOOK DIRECTIONS FOR "MIRROR"

Ingredients:

Two or more players; category sheets; mirror code sheets.

Basic Recipe:

1. Each player should have the appropriate code sheet. (This is determined by the version of the game that is being played.)

2. All group members should agree upon the categories that are to be used for the game. (There are a total of 15 categories. In some cases the group may decide to code only 6 or 7 categories.)

3. Each player should fill in the appropriate information on the coding sheets. (This includes the player's name and the names of all other group members.)

4. Each player should then go through each category and choose the most appropriate picture for each player, including himself. (for example, if a person feels that "red" is the color for Player A, he will record an "A" under category I—Color.)

5. After this process is completed, each player will take an individual summary sheet and record other's codes, along with his own self-codes. (This can be accomplished by passing the coding sheets around the group.)

Version I: Before and After

1. Follow steps 1-4, in the basic recipe for Mirror/rorriM, for the "Before" phase.

2. Decide upon a time (for example, the fourth meeting of the group) when the group will repeat this same process for the "After" phase.

3. After completing steps 1-4 for the "After" phase, each player should fill in a summary sheet for himself for the "Before" phase, and one for the "After" phase.

4. Discussion should center around the reasons involved with changes in perceptions from the "Before" to the "After" phase. (For example, did the players simply get to know each other better in terms of particular characteristics?)

Version II: The Silent Message

1. The group is instructed to limit all communication to nonverbal behavior.

2. The group performs a task, such as putting a puzzle together or baking cookies. (Facial expressions, touch, and body language can all be used to communicate the message.

3. The group then follows steps 1-5 in the basic recipe.

4. Discussion should focus on the particular nonverbal behaviors that contributed to the perception of a player by other players.

Version III: The Perfect Match

1. Players are divided into pairs. (These pairs could consist of "couples" or two men and two women. Ideally the partners in each pair should know one another fairly well.)

2. Each player begins recording on the "Couples Coding Sheet." (One player is Partner A and the other is designated as Partner B. Each partner records his self-codes and the codes for his partner.)

3. After this coding process is completed, the partners in each couple compile their codes on one sheet.

4. A point is awarded for each correct "match." (A correct match is identical coding between one partner's perception of himself, self-codes, and the codes by the other partner.)

Start Mixing at Slow Speed, Gradually Increasing. . .

The discussion following each game generally does not require a list of guidelines or questions. However, particular attention should be paid to (1) player's interpretations of the pictures, and (2) the reasons for selection of a particular picture for another player. This might involve the consideration of another player. This might involve the consideration of nonverbal behavior, verbal statements, or general appearance. The simple process of dealing with "what you think of others" can be very informative and also dangerous. SO "start mixing at slow speed, gradually increasing . . . ."

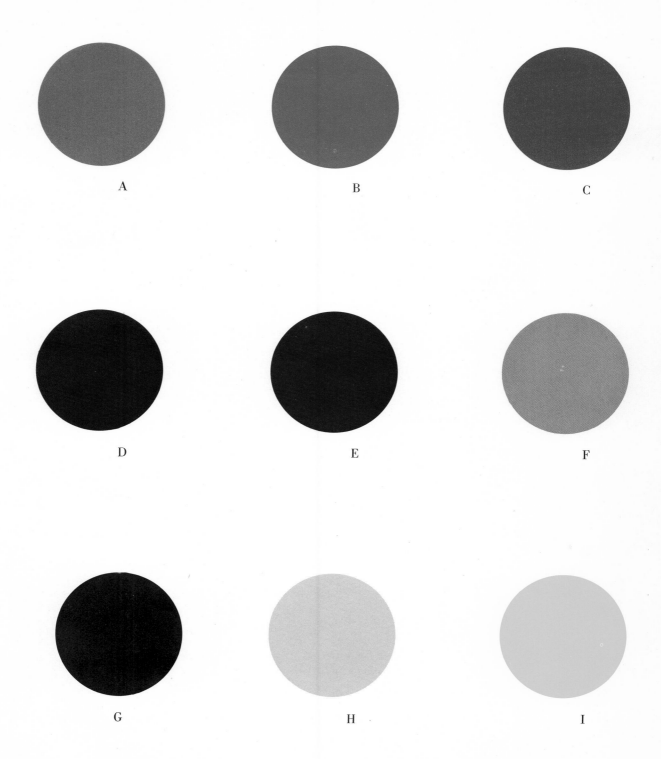

A

B

C

D

E

F

G

H

I

II.   SHADES OF COLORS
Choose a column of colors—A, B, or C

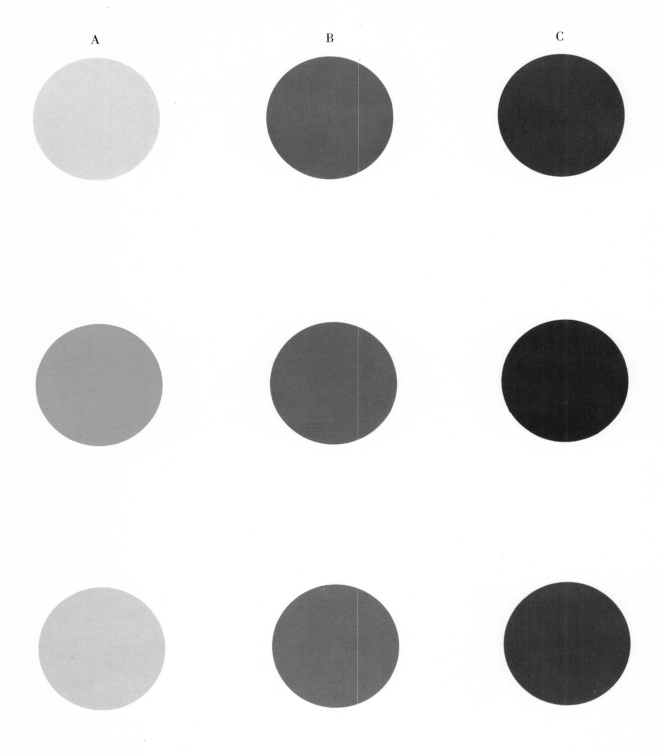

A

B

C

D

E

F

A

B

C

D

E

F

V. FRUITS

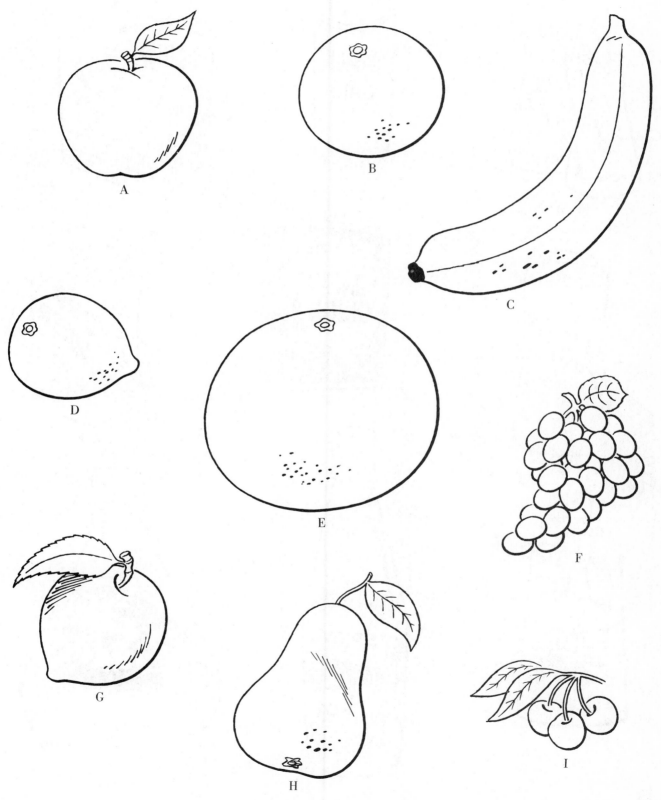

A

B

C

D

E

F

G

H

I

A

B

GARLIC
SALT

C

PAPRIKA

D

Allspice

E

MINCED
ONION

F

CURRY
POWDER

G

Cloves

H

SPICY
KETCHUP
HOT

I

Steak
Sauce

A

MAMA
Rosa's
PIZZA

CHING'S
CHINESE FOODS

B

LARRY'S
BAR AND GRILL

D

STEAK
and
LOBSTER
HOUSE

C

BIG
BURGER

F

POP'S
TRUCK STOP

E

A

B

C

D

E

F

A

B

C

D

E

F

A

B

C

D

E

F

A

B

C

D

E

F

A

B

C

D

E

F

GROUP CODING SHEET

for

Version I: Before and After
Version II: The Silent Message

Names	Category														
	I	II	III	IV	V	VI	VII	VIII	IX	X	XI	XII	XIII	XIV	XV
1. Self Code															
2.															
3.															
4.															
5.															
6.															
7.															
8.															
9.															
10.															

INDIVIDUAL SUMMARY CODING SHEET

for

Version I: Before and After
Version II: The Silent Message

Names	Category															
	I	II	III	IV	V	VI	VII	VIII	IX	X	XI	XII	XIII	XIV	XV
1.															
2.															
3.															
4.															
5.															
6.															
7.															
8.															
9.															
Summary Data: Most frequent response															
10.															

COUPLES CODING SHEET

for

Version III: The Perfect Match

Name									Category							
Partner A	I	II	III	IV	V	VI	VII	VIII	IX	X	XI	XII	XIII	XIV	XV
1. Self Codes															
2. "B" Codes															
Matches (X)															
Partner B	I	II	III	IV	V	VI	VII	VIII	IX	X	XI	XII	XIII	XIV	XV
1. Self Codes															
2. "A" Codes															
Matches (X)															

five communiquizzes

Judy L. Haynes

If you turned to this page expecting a *test* (a quiz on communication), you're in for a surprise. *Communiquizzes* are puzzles similar to the variety of puzzles found in crossword books. However, these puzzles have been written especially for communication students. There are five puzzles: two communicodes, two communiquotes, and a quiz on Signs of Approval.

The first Communiquote is below. Good luck!

communiquote 1

A communiquote is a quotation about communication. You can find out what the quotation is by answering the definitions and then transferring the letters to the blanks in the solution. The author of the quotation is below the quotation.

The word list is on page 45, and the solution is on page 63.

DEFINITIONS	WORDS
Dentures	$\overline{31}\ \overline{16}\ \overline{39}\ \overline{1}\ \overline{36}$
Very large	$\overline{20}\ \overline{13}\ \overline{28}\ \overline{3}$
T-bone or sirloin	$\overline{40}\ \overline{31}\ \overline{21}\ \overline{7}\ \overline{38}$
Perspiring	$\overline{30}\ \overline{6}\ \overline{25}\ \overline{10}\ \overline{1}\ \overline{17}\ \overline{11}\ \overline{15}$
Lovers' card	$\overline{24}\ \overline{14}\ \overline{9}\ \overline{34}\ \overline{18}\ \overline{19}\ \overline{22}\ \overline{11}\ \overline{29}$
Sweetener	$\overline{35}\ \overline{32}\ \overline{12}\ \overline{43}\ \overline{23}$
Need food; be _____	$\overline{2}\ \overline{32}\ \overline{18}\ \overline{28}\ \overline{4}\ \overline{27}$
Fix	$\overline{26}\ \overline{45}\ \overline{41}\ \overline{37}\ \overline{22}\ \overline{33}$
Cowboy movie	$\overline{6}\ \overline{42}\ \overline{8}\ \overline{19}\ \overline{5}\ \overline{44}\ \overline{11}$

SOLUTION:
$\overline{1}\ \overline{2}\ \overline{3}\ \overline{4}\ \overline{5}\ \overline{6}\ \overline{7}\ \overline{8}\ \overline{9}\ \overline{10}\ \overline{11}\ \overline{12}\ \overline{13}\ \overline{14}\ \overline{15}\ \overline{16}$

$\overline{17}\ \overline{18}\ \overline{19}\ \overline{20}\ \overline{21}\ \overline{22}\ \overline{23}\ \overline{24}\ \overline{25}\ \overline{26}\ \overline{27}\ \overline{28}\ \overline{29}\ \overline{30}\ \overline{31}\ \overline{32}\ \overline{33}\ \overline{34}$

$\overline{35}\ \overline{36}\ \overline{37}\ \overline{38}\ \overline{39}\ \overline{40}\ \overline{41}\ \overline{42}\ \overline{43}\ \overline{44}\ \overline{45}$

If you're still in the solving mood, there's another puzzle on page 63.

P–A–C
at work

Lyman K. Randall

Randall discusses a new way of looking at interpersonal interactions, called "transactional analysis." Read on and see if it helps you understand your own interpersonal communications a little more clearly.

1. KNOCK, KNOCK, WHO'S THERE?

When reality knocks at your door, who answers? A whining, complaining little boy or girl? A stern, scolding parent? Or a calm, alert adult? For example, suppose your boss tells you that he wants you to work overtime tonight and you have been planning for several weeks to meet some old friends for dinner immediately after work. Do you (a) turn to one of your colleagues and say, "Why do these things always happen to me, anyway? What's the use in making plans around here? He could have just as easily picked on somebody else." (b) Jump up from your chair and say to your boss, "That's not fair! You have no right to expect me to change my personal plans for this evening when you give me such short notice!" (c) reply to your boss, "That's going to cause a problem for me. You see, I've been planning for several weeks to meet some old friends tonight whom I haven't seen in 3 years. Is it possible to get someone else to work late tonight? Or perhaps I can come in early tomorrow morning. What do you think?"

Perhaps you can remember reacting to similar situations in each of these three different modes of behavior. They're called the Parent ego state, the Adult ego state, and the Child ego state. To simplify things, from now on we'll refer to these ego states as Parent, Adult, and Child with capital letters to distinguish them from actual parents, adults and children.

Recognizing your own Parent, Adult, and Child (or P-A-C for short) is the first step. But what are they? Where do they come from? How do you know one from the other when you see it?

In his book, *I'm OK, You're OK,* Dr. Tom Harris describes the experiments of Dr. Wilder Penfield, a Canadian neurosurgeon. Dr. Penfield, using an electrical stimulus, was able to trigger recorded speech and feelings that were stored like tape recordings in the patient's brain. Not only was the memory of an event recalled, but the whole experience was relived by the individual. For example, one individual not only recalled an early experience that involved her walking past a bakery, but she also began whistling a tune that she associated with the experience and reported actually smelling the aroma of freshly baked bread. The development of the three ego state concepts was, in part, based on these experiments. The Parent and the Child are permanent recordings in the brain. These tapes are never erased. They can, however, be up-dated by the Adult.

The Child: C

First, let's take a look at the Child. The Child in you is that body of data, recorded and stored in your brain when you were little. It comes from how you responded internally to what you saw and heard in the external world at that time. These recordings are primarily feelings and conclusions about yourself based on these feelings. They include feelings of frustration, inadequacy, and helplessness that were an inevitable part of your childhood. In addition, they contain the early recordings of joy, curiosity, imagination, spontaneity, and the excitement born from new discoveries which were also part of your childhood. For these reasons, the Child is often called the "felt concept of life."

In the example above, it was your Child who answered the knock of reality by pouting and sulking away from your boss after he asked you to work overtime. Your Child can be "hooked" by an event that generates strong feelings. You can spot your Child when you find yourself whining, sulking, throwing a tantrum, or abandoning yourself to the joy of a pleasurable new experience.

The Parent: P

Your Parent is that body of data, also recorded and stored in your brain, that comes from your observations about the way your mother and father (or other important "Big People" in your early life) behaved. It is based on external events that occurred essentially in the first five or six years of your life. It is a mosaic of learnings which you constructed as a little person that is captioned, "This is the way the world out there really is!" Because of your smallness and dependency as a little person in a world of "giants," your overriding assumption was that THEY were right. For these reasons, the Parent is often referred to as the "taught concept of life."

Your Parent was the part of you that responded to your boss by lecturing to him about what is or is not a fair and proper way to treat you. Your Parent lectures, moralizes, points its finger righteously or accusingly, teaches, and "lays down the law." You'll know your Parent is in charge when you find your scolding finger pointing, hear yourself lecturing about what's wrong (or right) about today's youth, or discover yourself correcting somebody's grammar or manners.

The Adult: A

Your Adult is that part of you that figures things out by collecting and looking at the facts. You may find it helpful to think of your Adult as your computer which you use to estimate probabilities and to make decisions based on facts. Everyone, even little children, has an Adult which is capable of making assessments about outside reality. For this reason, the Adult is sometimes called the "thought concept of life."

When you told your boss why working overtime would create a problem for you and suggested some alternatives for him to consider, your Adult had taken charge. Since everyone has the three ego states, once you learn to identify your own P-A-C it will be easy for you to recognize the P-A-C in others.

In some ways, our P-A-C's are like three different voices inside us. Our Parent is the voice that says things like: "You must . . . You ought to . . . You shouldn't . . . don't ever . . ." Our Parent tape plays back such old familiar recordings as: "If you want something done right, do it yourself . . . Big boys never cry . . . Idleness is the devil's playmate . . . A penny saved is a penny earned . . . etc."

Any time you find yourself talking to yourself (either out loud or under your breath) and using the word *YOU*, your Parent is very likely addressing your Child. For example, when you say to yourself, "That was a dumb thing for YOU to do," your Parent is scolding your Child.

Our Child is the voice that says: "I want what I want when I want it . . . Try and make me! . . . Wow! Great! . . . Drop dead! . . . etc." Any time you are experiencing feelings or emotions (happiness, sadness, fear, etc.) your Child is participating in the experience in some way.

Our Adult operates on facts based on what's true today. It is the voice within us which says things like: "What's going on here? . . . *Now* I see why this happened the way it did . . . What part of me came on just a few seconds ago—my Parent? Adult? or Child? . . . Why did I react just the way I did? . . . etc."

You can become acquainted with your own P-A-C by listening to these three different voices inside yourself. You may not always hear distinct words. Sometimes you will be able to decipher messages from the feelings bubbling up inside you. Naturally, you cannot hear the voices or directly experience the feelings occurring within other people. You can, however, become skilled in spotting the P-A-C in others (and yourself) by watching for the kinds of cues [shown in the chart]. The examples in this chart are only a few of the cues to watch for.

As you become more skilled in spotting these P-A-C cues in others, you will also become more aware of some of them in yourself. You can also get some cues from others about how you come across to them by identifying how they react to you. For example, suppose a customer reacts to something you have just said with, "Well, I was only trying to find out where I was supposed to catch my plane!" You might learn something about yourself by replaying what it was you said (or how you said it) immediately prior to the customer's hurting-complaining response. Possibly the customer thought you were "putting him down" or scolding him in some way. It is important to stress that everyone has P-A-C ego states operating. The goal of learning T.A. is to strengthen the Adult in each of us so that we can not only ask, but also answer, questions like: "What part of me is coming on? Are these data true, appropriate, and reasonable for *today's* reality?" To put it another way, T.A. provides us with a means of putting our Adult in the Living Room of today, ready to respond to the problems of daily living that knock on our "front door of life." This does not mean that we are to do away with our Parent and Child. It would be a dull world without them. It does mean, however, that we want to be free enough to be able to examine these two data-tapes.

To the extent that our Parent and Child tapes are archaic and unexamined, we will be dominated by the past. To the extent, however, we are able to learn the truth about how we behave, we will be free. Perhaps this is one of the meanings behind the old saying "Know the truth, and the truth will make you free."

2. COMING ON STRAIGHT, CROSSED AND CROOKED

Scene #1

Stewardess: "May I see your boarding pass?"

Passenger: (In angry tone) "I've already given my ticket to the man in the terminal!"

Scene #2

Employee: "I really would like to get your help in solving my lost time problem."

Supervisor: "OK. Why don't you get a thorough medical examination?"

Employee: "I've thought of that, but I don't have the money now."

Supervisor: "Why don't you try to get more sleep each night?"

Employee: "I've tried that, but my neighbors are too noisy." (etc.)

How many times have you found yourself in situations like the two scenes above? It is common for communication wires between people to get crossed in daily conversations. But why? How do these breakdowns in communication occur? And what can you do to untangle them? T.A. may have some ideas to help you.

In T.A., a *transaction* is an exchange of words and related behavior between two people. For example, when you say, "Good morning, Jim" and he says, "Good morning" back to you, you and Jim have completed a bit of social business which we have defined as a transaction.

When we see each person involved in the exchange as having a Parent, Adult, and Child, we are able to draw an accurate diagram of what happens in the transaction (thus the term, *transactional analysis*). The Parent, Adult, or Child in one person will always be answering the Parent, Adult, or Child in the other person. Any conversation is a series of transactions, one exchange

	Parent Ego State	Adult Ego State	Child Ego State
Voice Tones	Condescending, putting down, criticizing, or accusing	Matter-of-Fact	Full of feeling
Words Used	Everyone knows that . . . You should never . . . You should always . . . I can't understand why in the world you would ever . . .	How, What, When, Where, Why Who, Probable	I'm mad at you! . . . Hey, great (. . . or any words that have a high feeling level connected with them.)
Postures	Puffed-up, super-correct, very proper	Attentive, eye-to-eye contact, listening and looking for maximum data.	Slouching, playful, beat-down or burdened, self-conscious.
Facial Expressions	Frowns, worried or disapproving looks, chin jutted out.	Alert eyes, paying close attention.	Excitement, surprise, downcast eyes, quivering lip or chin, moist eyes.
Body Gestures	Hands on hips, pointing finger in accusation, arms folded across chest	Leaning forward in chair toward other person, moving closer to hear and see better.	Spontaneous activity, wringing hands, pacing, withdrawing into corner or moving away from laughter, raising hand for permission.

after another. Transactions can be Adult to Adult, Adult to Parent, Adult to Child, Parent to Parent, Parent to Adult, Parent to Child, Child to Parent, etc.

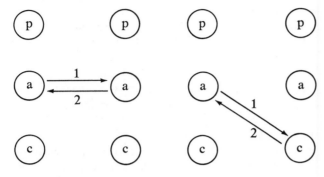

1. It's time to go.

2. I'm ready let's go.

1. You really look tired. May I help you with your baggage?

2. Whew! I'm exhausted! Thanks.

Examples #1 and #2 above are simple transactions. The arrows indicate who is saying what to whom. In each of these examples, the lines are parallel or uncrossed. As long as the lines in a transaction remain uncrossed, the conversation can go on indefinitely with no breakdown in communication. For this reason this type of exchange is called a complementary transaction.

Scene #1 is an example of a crossed transaction. When we diagram it, the transaction looks like this:

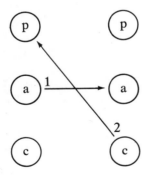

Stewardess
1. May I see your boarding pass?"

Passenger
2. "I've already given my ticket to the man in the terminal!"

In this example the Stewardess is using her Adult to ask the Adult of the passenger, "May I see your boarding pass?" Instead of responding with his Adult with something like "Yes, here it is," the passenger responds angrily with his Child, "I've already given my ticket to the man in the terminal." The passenger has reacted as if the Stewardess has made an unreasonable *demand* on

him from her parent when in reality she has not. The communication about the passenger giving the Stewardess his boarding pass has broken down. The transaction has become crossed. A second rule of communication is: Whenever the subject is abruptly diverted (rather than simply completed), look for a crossed transaction.

In this situation the Stewardess has a choice of response to this crossed transaction. She could scold the passenger with her Parent for being so gruff with her. Or she could react with her Child showing anger or hurt feelings. Or she could use her Adult again and give more information to the Adult of the passenger: "Yes, I'm certain you did, sir. However, the man inside gave you a blue or white piece of paper with your seat number written on it. That's your boarding pass which I'd like to see now." It is probable that the customer will respond with his Adult to this last stewardess comment. Thus the transaction is uncrossed and the business of showing the boarding pass can be completed.

Scene #2 is an example of a duplex transaction. When we diagram it, the transaction looks like this:

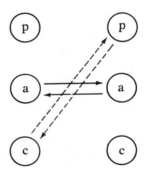

Employee
1. "I really would like to get your help in solving my lost time problem."

3. "I've thought of that, but I don't have the money now."

5. "I've tried that but my neighbors are too noisy."

Superior
2. "OK. Why don't you get a thorough medical examination?"

4. "Why don't you get more sleep each night?"

6. (etc.)

On the surface this series of transactions appears to involve an employee asking with his Adult for suggestions from his supervisor. And the supervisor, in turn, appears to be replying with ideas from his Adult. There is, however, a second, or hidden, psychological level of communication occurring. At this hidden psychological level the employee is saying, "I'm helpless to solve my own problems so I need a wise person (Parent) like you to solve them for me." The supervisor, in turn, responds on the psychological level with, "Yes I recognize my

33

wisdom and will be happy to give you advice." But then in the 3rd and 5th parts of the transaction, the employee rejects the advice that he appeared to be asking for.

If we look only at the surface or social level of this transaction, it won't make sense to us. It appears contradictory. If, however, we look at the hidden psychological level, we can begin to see that the basic purpose of the transaction was to *reject* advice rather than to receive it. By rejecting the ideas of the supervisor, the employee is able "to prove" his superiority over the boss in an underhanded or crooked way. This type of transaction is called a duplex transaction because it involves 2 levels of communication, an apparent social level and a hidden psychological level. Duplex transactions are commonly called games. . .

3. WORK IS NOT THE ONLY THING THAT OCCURS AT WORK

How many times have you heard, "You're expected to put in 8 hours of work in exchange for 8 hours of pay!" Work, however, is not the only thing that occurs on the job. People have six different ways to structure their time. Whether they are on the job or off makes little difference. These six time-structuring methods apply to all situations. They include (1) withdrawal, (2) rituals, (3) activities or "work," (4) pastimes, (5) games, and (6) authenticity or intimacy. Each of these approaches is related to the life position which you have taken.

The least risky way you can fill your time is *withdrawal*. You withdraw from people and situations when you are physically present by mentally putting yourself in another place or situation. Withdrawal is programmed by your Child as an escape from a boring or threatening present situation. It can also be a way of getting imaginary strokes from imaginary people through daydreams.

Rituals are the next safest way to fill your time and to get *strokes*. They are fixed ways of behaving towards other people which are programmed by your Parent. Rituals are closely related to good manners or "the proper thing to do when you're with others." For example, when you meet someone you know, usually you will say, "Hi! How are you today?" And the other person will likely say in return, "Fine. How are you?" This is a greeting ritual in which you give your friend several work strokes in return for several similar strokes from him. If you have good manners you will probably be a good stroker because you can be depended on to go through with rituals.

A third way you can fill your time is through *activities* which are often called work tasks. Activities are aimed at getting something done. For example,

writing an airline ticket, painting a house, writing a letter, or fixing and serving dinner are all activities. Since work is often done with or for other people, it is also a common way of getting or "earning" strokes. Play and recreation are also activities.

Pastimes are a fourth way you can fill your time. Some pastimes are programmed by your Adult to get more information about another person. A common example of this is, "What kind of work do you do?" Other pastimes are programmed by your Parent or your Child to get strokes from others. Examples of these include, "What did you think of the President's speech last night?" and "Have you heard the story about the drunk who . . ." If you have a deficiency of pastimes, you will often feel like a wallflower in social gatherings. Everyone else will be getting lots of strokes except you. Pastimes are usually pleasant and safe ways of exchanging strokes and getting to know people without getting too close to them.

Interpersonal games are a fifth way you can fill your time. Nearly all people play interpersonal games (not to be confused with recreational games) even though they really aren't much fun. Games are programmed by our Not OK Child to help it get strokes and deal with its Not OK feelings. The next section of this handbook will cover games in more detail.

Authenticity or intimacy is the sixth way you can fill your time with other people. Authenticity is programmed by your Adult and occurs when you are in the "I'm OK—You're OK" life position. It is a warm, caring, straight (non-game playing) series of transactions with another person. Authenticity is a means by which people really come together whereas the other five ways of filling time keep you at safe distances from others. In authenticity you are the most vulnerable because you are giving more of yourself away than at any other time.

Your own experience probably tells you that all six of these methods for filling time occur on the job as well as off. The more time you spend with an individual, the more likely you will use all six time-structuring methods. For example, a ticket salesman will probably use only rituals and activities with a customer since he spends so little time with him. On the other hand, a stewardess on a five hour non-stop flight may find that she is engaged in all six time-structuring methods with her passengers.

You can use your job in all six time-structuring ways described above. You can withdraw from relationships by losing yourself in your job. Work can provide you with many opportunities for stroke-exchanging rituals. All jobs are primarily focused on activities designed to get certain things done. Your job also provides you with frequent opportunities for pastimes that help you get to know other people better and exchange recognitions with them. Your job can also serve as a playing field for games. And finally your job can provide you with opportunities for authentic relationships with colleagues and sometimes even customers. Work, therefore, is not the only thing that occurs at work . . . .

"This smokeless fuel the anti-pollution people make us use is killing the art of communication!"

CAUTION!
conversation being demolished

This article describes "Cute Kids," "haters," "irrational rationalizers," and other types who help destroy conversations — you may have met some of them already.

Kaye Starbird

The first law of discussion, it seems,
is that if there's any possible way
to derail the train of thought,
somebody will

I like a good discussion as well as the next person. But over the years I have come to recognize that the premise of even the simplest oral exchange can get lost in a tangle of side issues and individual interpretations. On such occasions, I am reminded of the time I went to church as a child, and we sang that hymn entitled "Gladly the Cross I'd Bear." While the grown-ups in the congregation were picturing the long road to Calvary, I, like many another child before me, was visualizing a big furry animal with a strange name and an unfortunate ocular problem—Gladly, the crosseyed bear.

I cite this incident to demonstrate how the spoken word can give rise to varying misconceptions, which often complicate further conversation to the point of absurdity. One classic example of this difficulty, which I call Proceeding Reasonably From a Wrong Premise, occurred shortly after World War II when a beau of mine named Homer Hoskins appeared at the house.

I came downstairs to find Homer talking with my father, a retired Army general, in the living room. They were discussing what everyone had done during the war. Somewhat defensively, Homer announced that he had been a conscientious objector. But he didn't use the term "conscientious objector." He simply said that he had spent the previous 19 months as a C.O. out on the West Coast.

There was a moment of silence. Then my father, delighted, slapped his knee and said he thought the occasion called for a drink. I couldn't understand his uncharacteristic reaction, until I suddenly remembered that C.O. meant Commanding Officer in Army parlance; my father had automatically accepted the abbreviation in the context familiar to him. "At your age," he kept saying approvingly. "At your age."

Somewhat puzzled at first, Homer gained confidence over a couple of congratulatory brandies and explained that each man had to do what he believed in and serve according to his own capacities and instincts to help attain peace. My father said: True, true; any army officer worth his salt knew that. Whereupon Homer said he was glad my father realized how trying his position had sometimes been; it wasn't easy for a man to isolate himself from the companionship of most of his friends and acquaintances. My father nodded. Being a C.O. was a damned lonely business, he agreed. Damned lonely.

I was perspiring profusely in my concern with what would happen when the two of them got down to details. In a flurry of fake femininity and contrived excuses, I whisked Homer off to the movies.

The People Who Proceed Reasonably From a Wrong Premise are not the only ones to muddy the crystal waters of conversation. There are also the Cute Kids, the Haters, the Monologuists, the Irrational Rationalizers and the Premise Shifters. The Cute Kids, Haters and Monologuists have a lot in common. They listen for words rather than meanings, restlessly waiting for an opportunity to thrust their own humor, vituperation or opinionated reminiscence into the first vocal opening. A Cute Kid will say anything for laughs. If everyone in the room is talking about whether or not Tennessee Williams is a great playwright, a Cute Kid will say that he always liked *A Streetcar Named Desire,* but there ought to be an Irish version of it called *The Rose of Trolley.*

A Hater, on the other hand, is mainly on the alert for proper names that will give him a chance to vilify someone. He can make do with a limited vocabulary.

The talk can be about Whistler's Mother, Albert Schweitzer or the high-school janitor, and he will suddenly pound his fist on whatever's handy and snort: "That s.o.b.!" There is no use trying to converse seriously with a Cute Kid or Hater present. Or a Monologuist either, for that matter.

My grandmother was a great Monologuist. In nothing flat, she could bring even the most well-channeled conversation around to the subject of the Old West. I remember one afternoon when she was serving tea to two elderly Monologuist contemporaries, a Mr. McDillip and his wife. My grandmother started off by saying what a cold winter it was, and Mr. McDillip said Yes, it was almost as cold as the winter of '81 when his house burned in Maine. My grandmother said she guessed she had been out in the Old West that year; and Mrs. McDillip said her rheumatism was bothering her again; it always did in cold weather. Mr. McDillip said it was 20 below zero when his house caught fire in Maine. At around 11 p.m. he had smelled smoke and had yelled like an Indian. My grandmother said she had got pretty accustomed to Indians out in the Old West, although she had to admit she'd been a bit leery of them when the Colonel first married her and took her to Fort Laramie. Sometimes, she was left alone in the house with Annie the cook and an orderly who was too crippled to be of much use. Mrs. McDillip sympathized with the crippled orderly. Some mornings she could scarcely move, she said. Of course, she had her new heating pad, but it was hard to regulate the heat. Heat! said Mr. McDillip. Nobody ever felt anything like the heat from the burning kitchen the night he and his parents and two younger brothers hurried through the hallway in their bathrobes out into the freezing weather...And so it went, all afternoon, the three of them carrying on their monologues quite amicably in the naive belief that they were communicating with one another.

Monologuists are at least predictable. Unfortunately, the same thing can't be said for Irrational Rationalizers. Teen-agers are practiced Irrational Rationalizers and are inclined to take rather a patronizing attitude toward anyone who fails to comprehend. As a mother, I call this Oatmeal Logic.

When my oldest daughter, Kit, was 14, she used to fill her cereal bowl at breakfast with great mounds of cereal which she never ate. "Why do you take all that oatmeal every morning?" I asked her one day.

"If I don't have a lot of oatmeal," she answered, "I start to feel faint before noon."

"Yes, but you never eat it," I pointed out.

"I never have time," she said

"Well, if you never have time to eat the cereal," I

went on, refusing to let well enough alone, "why do you put so much in your bowl?"

"I told you," she replied witheringly. "If I don't have a lot of oatmeal in the morning, I start to feel faint before noon."

The Premise Shifters are another devious breed. I have a sister who is an accomplished one. The other night she was saying she couldn't understand why I had sent my daughters to the local Country Day School. Public school had been good enough for her, she said, and it was important for kids to be brought up in a democratic atmosphere and not be snobs. I explained that the school was excellent and had a well-endowed scholarship fund which enabled students from any social or economic background to attend. There was a plumber's daughter enrolled, a policeman's son, a hairdresser's son, and my cleaning woman's oldest girl, who was very talented musically. That was all very well, my sister said, but what baffled her was why I wanted my children in with that bunch of beatniks in the first place. When I suggested that we were talking about snobs, my sister said I was trying to evade the issue.

When you get an assortment of these types together, it's hopeless attempting to discuss *anything* in an orderly manner. Yesterday at a cocktail party, a friend of mine mentioned that he had recently got over a bad bout of Asian flu, which had affected his motor reflexes. A woman near him, Proceeding Reasonably from a Wrong Premise, said she had trouble driving a car, too. She added that she was going to have to take another driver's test soon, and she hoped the examiner wouldn't be too exacting. One of the Haters present happened to know the examiner—an s.o.b. if he'd ever met one—who held his job only because he was a nephew of the mayor (another s.o.b). A lurking Premise Shifter managed to parlay the subsequent listing of the mayor's personality faults into an appraisal of the downtown traffic problem—a situation which a listening female Irrational Rationalizer seemed to feel was in some way responsible for the poor architecture on Main Street. The North Country bank was bad enough, she said, but the sight of the new bus terminal actually made her ill. A Cute Kid leapt on this statement to chortle something about "terminal illness"; and a sleepy-eyed Monologuist philosopher, abruptly coming alive, commented on the brevity of our sojourn in this vale of tears and commenced a rambling dissertation on the Life to Come.

As I disengaged myself from the group, I had one fleeting thought: I don't know much about the Eternal Life, but in a conversation like this, Life Here and Now can sometimes *seem* eternal.

Meet someone halfway.
To communicate is the beginning of understanding. AT&T

Getting Un-Crossed Up

Bernard Gunther*

It seems that there are two schools of thought regarding the healing of mental, emotional, and spiritual problems. The Western therapeutic approach often ignores the spiritual aspects of being.† For all its theoretical variations, it concentrates on the understanding, reexperiencing, and releasing of old traumas, destructive behavior patterns, and emotional blocks. The advocates of this psychotherapeutic method insist that you must fully relive and express past emotions and events before they can be eliminated from your consciousness. The problem is that the task is endless. Often it is not effective and, in fact, can reinforce by getting a person stuck in his lower destructive forces. This can be extremely painful, not only for the patient, but for all those around him.

The Eastern or metaphysical approach is to let go of the past, to enter fully into the here and now, to move above the physical-emotional forces and into the clear, blissful, compassionate detachment of the superconscious self. Don't stir the mud; let it settle. The symbol of the lotus which has its roots in the mud and its stem in the water, floats above them, basking in the warm light of the eternal sun. The methods used in this approach vary from master to master; there is an infinite number of schools or points of view. To various degrees, they all have their special forms of meditation, affirmation, chants, exercises, and disciplines.

The real truth of the matter is that, to some extent, both the Eastern and Western approaches work, and in fact, some people get results without doing anything. The explanation lies as much with natural growth, faith, belief, and luck, as with effort or the particular system you follow. It is a matter of finding *your own way* out of the hypnosis, conditioning, habit patterns, and suggestion that have split you off from your deeper self.

We live in a culture that through verbal indoctrination and nonverbal implication isolates almost every being from himself, nature, and others.* The Western child is forced to swallow the symbolic rotten apple of separation; and so this unsuspecting being is seduced out of innocent unity and into a so-called reality where he is

---

*Bernard Gunther is one of the pioneers in the use of touch, relaxation, meditation, and nonverbal communication in the total growth process. For seven years he was a staff member of the Esalen Institute at Big Sur. Many of his innovations are now being used in educational, religious, and therapeutic situations throughout the United States and Europe. He is the director of the feature film *Come to Your Senses,* and the author of *Sense Relaxation, Love View, What to Do Till the Messiah Comes,* and *How the West is One,* all published by Macmillan–Collier.

†The Psychosynthesis of Roberto Assagioli is a rich, rare exception.

*This is not a glorification of Eastern culture which has its own extraordinary and profound problems, along with a lack of physical-economic balance. The intent is, rather, to maintain that on the whole, Easterners, in their philosophy and way of life, are more in touch with the underlying unity of the universe.

Bernie Gunther wrote this piece for you and me. It reflects a unique approach to intrapersonal communications that is not often considered in Western cultures.

Read the piece and think about its message before you evaluate it. Either way, why not write Bernie and let him know your feelings about it?

Send your reactions to me, c/o Dept. of Communication, Florida State University, Tallahassee, Fla. 32306 — and I'll forward them to Bernie, wherever he may be at the time.

cut off from his true inner divine nature. A huge percentage of our population is more than half dead, living largely in its emotional solar plexus and verbal head without any real sense of its own uniqueness, aliveness, or power. The abusive use of alcohol, drugs, sex, and violence is symptomatic of this inner alienation. The shutting off of individuality and vitality has been carried to such a degree that many people freeze their existence into a dull series of still photographs rather than experience the exciting, dynamic, full, living-color, sound, taste, smell, and feeling, intuitive moving picture called life.

An important addition to this basic mis-i-dentification is that we live in a society in which the cultural hero is a man *hung-up* on a cross, suffering and dying for the supposed sins of humanity. Since this being exemplifies the highest ideal to be attained, we all try in some way to emulate his behavior. Unfortunately, without realizing it, we unconsciously get sucked into his misery rather than into the actions of his virtues—for the symbol is more powerful than all our preaching and verbal understanding. What this means is that without being aware of it, we consider pain, suffering, and failure as inevitable, integral parts of our life. After all, "it was good enough for the son of God." Our mistake is that we do not really comprehend the Christ legend. Christ is not a personality, but rather that higher aspect of consciousness that each of us possesses in our innermost self. The importance is not in the *hung-up* Jesus, but in the resurrection of the Christ-consciousness. The task is to transcend the suffering we all *go through,* come off it, and move up to this God-consciousness that is who we are. Such a rebirth is not just a return to child*ish* oneness, but the finding of a higher child*like* unity based on relatedness and overunderstanding. The fool of the Tarot, the wild card, who is *in* but not *of* the deck, is able to play any role because he knows that he is not really any of them. This is rebirth, the return to the joyous, compassionate Spirit Source, the next level of the journey homeward.

On the surface, most of us are aware of how this suffering symbol has been used to hold power, control behavior, and keep the masses in ignorance. What we fail to realize is the inner game *we play with ourselves.* As children, we learn very early how much sympathy and attention we can get when we feel bad. This is a most useful weapon in avoiding undesirable situations, excusing ourselves, and manipulating others. For pain, suffering, and disease are our culture's most acceptable excuses. We hang on to our misery and self-torture as if it were our most cherished possession, as if we had nothing better to live for or with. The truth of the matter is that we are afraid of that God-like part of ourselves, that aspect which is health, happiness, love,

and creativity. This can be best expressed by the popular statement "It's too good to be true." No matter how bad things are, most people accept them as inevitable: "That's life." Nobody ever says "It's too bad to be true."

Part of the dilemma is our collective and individual negativity and guilt: "We are born in sin," "God will punish you," or "You are a bad boy or girl." It was never made clear to you that what you did may have been bad or inconvenient for the adults that shared your environment, but that in spite of anything you do, you are a child of the nameless God, a God of love, not wrath.

One other part of the problem is that we are so used to feeling below par that it seems unnatural to feel good. We live in a time where health is equated with not being sick. This is a great deterrent to optimum behavior and creative change—for what is new is unfamiliar, and what is unfamiliar feels strange and not quite right.

Another source of our predicament is a game we learned to play as children; the game was called "Let's pretend." Once we learned the game, we not only played it with our playmates, but we began to play it with ourselves, our parents, our acquaintances, society, and the universe. It seemed to work so well that we carried it to the second power and made the game "Let's pretend and pretend that we're not pretending." We became so immersed in the game that we forgot to remember that we were pretending. This process evolves unconsciously to a point where we become lost and feel the need to go to a wise man, magician, guru, teacher, or a psychiatrist to get *un-crossed up:* REMEMBERED.

The term "magician" is not used here in a derogatory fashion, but as a means of expressing the true nature of the real mythological events that take place. The magician is a very high card in the Tarot deck, and a good sorcerer is a being of great power, knowledge, and, often, wisdom. The point is that because of his understanding, high energy vibration, and prestigious position, you give him the power to help you to *remember yourself.* For truly, no one else can heal you. The natural process that allows wholeness and regeneration is nowhere except within your very own being. Also, when you really get right down to it, you can never fully explain what happened. At best, you can observe and theorize about some of what has taken place. What it amounts to is that whether you use drugs, words, hypnosis, faith, behavior modification, Gestalt, or meditation, it is all magic: the transmutation of energy, the various elixirs of life. To explain this a little further, let us take walking as an example. Although you can describe it in endless detail, you can never really fully express how you do it—like the process of birth, breathing, and growing your hair, it just happens. Knowing how to control or to make some things happen with great predictability is called science; but ultimately we don't know how it happens—it is magic.

Much of the time, the process of healing has to do with faith, the belief in one's self, another person, or some power. Time also is an important factor, because things do not seem to take place until they are ready to happen or until we are ready to let them happen. Here again, it is not a question of one method working and another not, but rather which methods work most effectively for you. Some methods are surely more consistent and effective than others; penicillin, in most cases, works faster than sulfa and with fewer side effects.

Moving back to our original question: Is it necessary or as efficient to go through all the psychic mud in order to move up to the open spaces above the mental, emotional waters? The answer is, of course, individual, but it seems that the path of letting the mud settle and moving up into the sun offers less struggle with more positive, lasting results, more contact with the spiritual self and the source of the universe.

Now even though in all the Zen stories, all of this seems to take place in a flash, it usually requires a shift of attitude, the understanding and following of certain universal laws, plus a substantial degree of self-discipline: observing your thoughts and keeping them in a constructive, positive direction; letting go of past experiences, and retaining only the wisdom gained; not being controlled by your emotions or physical desires; breathing in a deep, rhythmic, flowing manner; and taking conscious control of your mind. Assuming responsibility for the choices you make, identifying with the spiritual source of your consciousness, and dedicating your every act to it represents a personal living philosophy of life that is the essence of the Bible, meditation, and all religion. This is a code of behavior and awareness—a spiritual interconnection that is in functional harmony with your deeper self and the rest of the universe.

So, away from the tragic and into the magic, the dance of molecular matter in the infinite space of eternal time, the joy-play of universal mind—the source of the cosmos, pretending that it is lonely, separate, afraid, and lost. For in the super-real reality of unity, it is the ultimate game, the evolutionary Odyssey, all and everything, ultimately remembering itself in the divine laughter of loving bliss.

The Short Unhappy Life of the Boy Who Wouldn't Listen

Joseph Zaitchik

This is a modern fairy tale. However, it does not begin with "Once upon a time," and, come to think of it, the ending is not "happily ever after," either. Read on and see what I mean.

Uggle blug blug uggle, he said. Don't you bluggle me, his mother told him. When I talk to you listen when I talk to you. She gave him the back of her hand. Listen when I talk to you listen.

Uggle blug, he muttered.

She pulled his hair. You stop that, she said, when I talk to you stop that.

Bluggle uggle blug! he thought, thinking very hard, clenching fists and teeth and eyes, making a terrible face.

I know what you're thinking, she said, and she gave him the back of her hand. Don't you bluggle me when I'm talking to you don't you bluggle me.

He tried it again, this time very lightly, thinking very quietly, barely touching the thought: *Uggle . . .*

She didn't know.

He tried again, looking at her now, facing her, looking her straight in the eye, thinking just a little bit harder, but still calmly, still quietly, still not showing it on his face: *Uggle . . . . bluggle . . . . blug . . . .*

She made a face, but she didn't know.

Again, just a wee bit stronger, faster: *Blug uggle buggle . . .*

She looked at his face and she made a face. But she didn't know. She grabbed his wrist and pulled him after her down the avenue, talking, talking.

He didn't hear a word. *Uggle,* he went, *uggle blug bluggle uggle blug glubble . . .*

He was eight when he learned that trick. Look them straight in the eye, never mind what they say, just go bluggle in your head, not too hard, not too loud, and you won't hear a word they're saying. It was a great discovery.

By the time he was twelve he was an expert. He could do almost anything while he bluggled—give you a great big smile, light a cigarette, nod his head like you're so right, hum a little tune, just about anything. And all the time he didn't hear a word, all he heard was bluggling in his head. Even if it was a cop. It was a big advantage. People had to listen to you, but you didn't have to listen to them. Not if you didn't like what they were saying. And nobody could figure out how you did it, what the secret was. And sometimes it just about drove them crazy sometimes.

For example, in school, he could stand right there in front of the hawk-nosed, red-faced principal, and watch those thin blue lips moving as fast as anything—and it was like watching TV when something goes wrong with the sound on the TV. Funny. Once he laughed it was so funny—and that's when he learned something else. Laughing stopped the bluggling, you can't bluggle while you laugh you can't bluggle. A laugh is open, a bluggle is closed. A laugh, a real one, opens the closed. You just can't relax when you bluggle, you got to keep your mind on the bluggles, you relax even a little and pretty soon you're hearing the words and you're listening to what they mean and you get mad as anything. You can't bluggle when you're mad as anything. That's another thing: when you get mad, after you get mad, it comes out different. The it goes *groogle yoogle grug groogle yoogle grug* it goes, and it's noisy inside, like starting up the car and giving it all that loving gas, and when it starts going like that, *groogle yoogle grug groogle yoogle grug,* you got to be very careful when it starts going like that. Groogles are very easy to lose. Like the time he laughed, and his head opened up and he lost the bluggles, and he grabbed the groogles and it got so noisy inside he lost the groogles, and he jumped over the principal's desk and slugged him in the teeth.

And that was another great discovery: you can groogle with your hands. If you're too tired to bluggle, or if you're nervous and you start sweating like anything, or if you feel like you're getting mixed up, then you just let the groogle start up inside, let it run for a few seconds until it gets nice and hot and noisy, and then you let it out through your hands.

Even your feet sometimes. Feet could groogle. He learned that the day he turned sixteen, and the cop put the handcuffs on him, and the groogling inside was giving him a big headache, and how could he groogle with his hands when the lousy things were bluggled behind his back? So he groogled with his feet he groogled. Beautifully.

By the time he was eighteen he could write a book, he figured he was ready to teach. So one day he was sitting in a room with some other guys, drinking beer and smoking, and he was telling them what was right and what was wrong, and that the fat guy who was the boss did everything wrong, and that don't worry pretty soon he'd be giving orders instead of taking them from the fat guy sleeping in the next room who you just wait and see would soon be sleeping for a long time.

Only the fat guy wasn't sleeping, and also the door was open a crack, and the fat guy came running out without his shoes on, and mad as anything. Listen here, you punk—

Bluggle uggle bluggle blug. He didn't hear a word.

The fat guy's face was real funny, like when something goes wrong with the sound on the TV, and the guy on the commercial is waving his arms around like mad and his mouth is going up and down about that deodorant, only you don't hear a word. Real funny, but he didn't laugh though, just kept on bluggling.

It was getting harder though, he couldn't keep that big smile going, the cigarette smoke was getting in his eyes, he couldn't concentrate, the beer was making it hard to concentrate. The bluggles started coming slower, not connected, leaving spaces. Words were coming through.

xxxxxxxxxxxxxxxxxxxx another thing xxxxxxxxxxxxxxxxxxxxxxxxxxxxxxxxxxxxx big trap xxxxxxxxxxxxxxxxxxxxxxxxxxxxxxx last time xxxxxxxxxxx lousy bone xxxxxxxxxxxxx

He thought with all his strength, clenched fist and teeth and eyes, put everything he had in it. *Bluggle! Uggle! Bluggle!*

xxxxxxxxxxxxxxxxxxxxxxxxxx end up at the bottom of the xxxxxxxx

No good. The guy was talking too fast, too loud. He switched from bluggle to groogle. *Groogle yoogle grug groogle yoogle grug...*

Fine. Good. The motor inside was hot and noisy, burning plenty of gas. He didn't hear a word. But then the fat guy grabbed him by the lapels and lifted him out of the soft chair and shook every last groogle out of him.

Then his hands went groogle. And when his hands were bluggled, he groogled with his feet.

And finally he couldn't even think with his feet. And soon he wasn't where he was before, he was outside somewhere, lying on the ground somewhere, all tied up, and the words he heard were as cold and sharp as the wind. He begged then, pleading his youth, weeping his remorse, communicating his regret.

Please, he said, give me a break, I'll do anything, just give me a break—

Bluggle uggle bluggle, went the fat guy.

Please, he begged, he wept, please listen to me, don't just stand there and bluggle—

Groogle yoogle grug! went the fat guy.

He couldn't stand it. He could hear the fat guy's groogles. He wouldn't listen any more. *Bluggle uggle blug!* he screamed.

Groogle yoogle grug! screamed back the fat guy.

Buggle groogle uggle yoogle grug blug boogle groogle— and suddenly he was lifted high in the air, and thrown; and he was falling, falling, and the wild wind tore the final groogle from his mouth, and he struck the hard, cold wetness, and all around was sound, cold-wet sound, and the cold was deafening, the wet too loud to hear. But then, descending, he began to hear, clearer and clearer, more and more familiar, descending with the sound, slowly wet and cold and clear:

Bruggle urgle burble glurg
Glurgle glurb blub
Urgle blug
gurgle
bubble
!glug!

When you consider that Kirkendall wrote this article in 1959, you've got to give him credit for being "with it." However, at this point in time the piece is probably more interesting than infor-mative. Relevant? Yes.

Semantics and Sexual Communication

Lester A. Kirkendall

Experience in research on sexual behavior and years of work in sex education and personal counseling have convinced me that we face important semantic difficulties when we try to improve understanding about sexual matters. Our language, the words we use, and the definitions we employ reflect our feelings, our concepts, and our scope of knowledge. This is true of sex as well as anything else.

When we lack words to express minute variations and subtle differences, when words simply reinforce our prejudices, or when our attitudes permit us to express ourselves in a circumscribed fashion only, communication is hampered and ineffective. This in turn interferes with clear understanding. Communication difficulties concerning sex arise from at least four conditions.

1. WORDS WHICH DESCRIBE THE DEGREE OR QUALITY IN SEXUAL BEHAVIOR ARE FEW

The word "intercourse" is used to describe all heterosexual congress, and sometimes homosexual association as well. A sexual contact with a prostitute is intercourse; so is a sexual relationship between a loving husband and wife. A sexual association entered in a spirit of bravado or hostility is equated, so far as terminology is concerned, with one entered with an attitude of affectionate sharing, or in an earnest desire to procreate. Yet, qualitatively speaking, these are very different experiences.

"Copulation" might be a better term to denote those associations which represent simply a genital union and a physical release. "Intercourse" could

45

then be reserved for associations which represent an interchange and a sharing of feelings between the partners. This distinction would mean that two persons could have "copulation" at will, but that "intercourse" would have to be achieved. Many persons, even among the married, who say they have had intercourse have experienced only copulation. Just because a person is sexually experienced is no proof that he has had intercourse.[1]

All sexual associations are referred to as "relationships" and the participants as "partners." Actually the words "contact" or "episode" much more appropriately describe casual, transitory associations, and the participants are more nearly "opponents" or "protagonists" than they are "partners."

All male-female sexual unions before marriage are referred to as "premarital intercourse." The only reason for this designation is that the persons involved are unmarried. A great many of these associations are "pre-" nothing; they are simply "nonmarital copulations." When the motivations in some of these experiences are examined they are clearly "anti-marital" associations. Sex may be used to block or ward off marriage as well as to anticipate it. The only genuine "premarital intercourse" would seem to be between those unmarried persons who genuinely love and respect each other, and who truly anticipate marriage.[2]

2. A LACK OF KNOWLEDGE CONCERNING THE NATURE AND SIGNIFICANCE OF VARIOUS ASPECTS OF SEX LEADS TO SEMANTIC DIFFICULTIES

The difficulty of ignorance about the various aspects of sex is implicit in some of the illustrations given above, but others can be added. One is found in our use of the words "homosexual" practices. Many people were astounded and greatly worried over data appearing in the first Kinsey Report showing that about forty percent of all males had had "homosexual" experiences. "Homeosexuality" means to these people an unalterable fixation and an abhorrent practice. Actually the Kinsey figures are as high as they are because they include "early adolescent genital play" between members of the same sex. Few individuals engaging in such genital play are fixated homosexuals; they are uninformed and curious about sex, and are expressing their interest in ways common to their age and developmental level.

The word "masturbation" is a blanket term which confuses, and many times, frightens people. Adults masturbate; so do young children. When the word is applied to both groups, the interpretation is that the same kind of behavior is being described. Actually small children usually engage in genital manipulation, play, or fondling, rather than masturbation. Adult masturbation may represent an occasional, chance experience, or it may be a deeply fixated practice. Here again we need words which will distinguish some of these very important differences.[3]

"Sex drive" is another term which has no clearly defined usage. To some it is a biological manifestation conditioned by hormonal conditions. To others it represents a psychological impulse toward sexual expression. Almost always when the term is used in relation to behavior it implies motivation.

As I pointed out in some earlier writing, "sex drive" is the expression often used when "sexual performance" is being discussed. "Sex drive" is said to vary greatly from individual to individual (as it does), but this is probably much more a psychological than a physiological difference. The real physiological difference is probably in "capacity" for sexual response rather than in "drive." So far as behavior is concerned, motivation seemingly determines "sex drive" rather than drive being a motivation in itself.

When we are able to determine clearly how "sexual performance" and "sexual capacity" are related to "sex drive" and work with all three of these interrelated concepts, we will have improved the semantic understanding of sex.[4] Lack of agreement on definition is at the bottom of some semantic difficulties, for example, the use of the word

---

[1] Readers of George Orwell's *1984* will recall that one of the primary objectives of the ruling clique was to see that everyone thought as he "ought" to think. To this end, a new language was developed in which words which might lead to heretical thoughts were eliminated, and the possibility of choosing among words was cut to a minimum. Since sex was to be thought about as little as possible and then only in the prescribed way, sexual communication, for all practical purposes, was limited to two words. All disapproved sexual acts were covered with one word: "sexcrime." "Goodsex" encompassed normal intercourse within marriage for procreation. Only "goodsex" was approved.

[2] For an elaboration of the points made in this and the preceding paragraphs see my book, *Premarital Intercourse and Interpersonal Relationships* (New York: Julian Press, 1961).

[3] For a valuable analysis of attitudes toward masturbation, see Lester W. Dearborn, "The Problem of Masturbation," *Marriage and Family Living,* XIV (February 1952), 46-55.

[4] See Lester A. Kirkendall, "Toward a Clarification of the Concept of Male Sex Drive," *Marriage and Family Living,* XX (November 1958), 367-372. Also dealing with this subject is a chapter in *The Encyclopedia of Sexual Behavior,* ed. Albert Ellis and Albert Abarbanel, II (New York: Hawthorne Books, 1961), 939-948.

masturbation as already noted. Homosexuality, which may also be called "inversion," "homogenic love," "homoeroticism," "contrasexuality," and still other terms, is a case in point...

3. A POWERFUL NEED TO DISPLAY DELICACY AND TO BE DIFFIDENT ABOUT SEX LEADS TO SEMANTIC CONFUSIONS

In our culture, we are perhaps moving somewhat from under the shadow of the problem of taboo words. The evidences of taboo are still present, however. Thus the genital organs are referred to as "the private parts." Or we are likely to refer to two persons who have had a sexual connection as having been "intimate." Certainly there is nothing intimate about most casual copulations, unless it is that the two have exposed the genital parts of their bodies to each other. Such phrases as "physical relationship" or "physical expression" have been used so persistently as euphemisms for "sexual intercourse" that embracing, petting, stroking, kissing, which are also physical relationships or expressions are never connoted by these phrases. There is also the implication that sex has none but a physical side.

Only in recent years have we been able to use the word "pregnant" openly. Formerly such expressions as "in the family way" or "a delicate condition" were used. "Menstruation" was another taboo word, and the substitute expressions commonly had a frightening tone about them: "the curse," "bleeding," "sick." The words "monthly" or "period" are less frightening but just as evasive. Everyone can remember when venereal diseases had to be referred to as "social diseases." The blanket expression "sexual offense" shields the hearer from any disturbing information as to what actually took place...

Actually we have several categories of sex language. Each expresses a particular purpose and each fulfills, at least in part, a specific need. Yet because of the intense feelings of reticence and the marked inhibitions which surround sex, these languages never quite mesh or interlock, as, for example, when a doctor talks to an uneducated patient, or a teacher or minister to a group of young people. As a consequence they are unable to bridge the chasm which the separate categories of language have created between themselves and the persons they wish to help...

4. JUDGMENTAL ATTITUDES ARE REFLECTED IN SEMANTIC DIFFICULTIES

Evidences of the difficulty of judgmental terms are all about us, too, though certainly less so than formerly. Sexual deviations are less often referred to as "perversions"—which connotes a willful turning away from the right. Masturbation has been "self-abuse" or the "solitary sin," while nocturnal emissions have been regarded as "corruptions." Sometimes our judgmental terms, loaded with scorn and rejection, injure innocent parties. Children born out of wedlock are sometimes "bastards" or possibly "children of sin." At the best they are likely to be "illegitimate children."[5]

Masculine aggressiveness and feminine passivity in the intercourse relationship is reflected in the verbs found in the folk vocabulary. For example, girls (women) are "taken," "had," "laid," "made," "punched out," "screwed." Some of these terms, the last two in particular, appear to bear overtones of disrespect and disdain—feelings which too often characterize nonsexual associations between men and women. Here, however, a class distinction doubtless needs to be made. Lower-class persons probably use these folk terms more naturally and as a reflection of what they regard as the normal roles of the sexes than do upper-class persons. Disrespect and disdain might be suspected particularly when the folk terms are used by persons who customarily use technical and scientific terms.[6]

I would like to suggest three possible steps which should improve our capacity for sexual communication.

Particular attention should be given to the language we use in expressing our sexual attitudes and beliefs. What are we actually saying? What assumptions are we making, and what feelings are we expressing? For example, why is it always "wife swapping" and never "husband swapping"? Once we are thus able to attend to our speech, certain confusions and contradictions will become obvious. The next challenge is how to resolve them.

Freedom for interchange and open discussion should be developed, especially in those situations which will bring groups now commonly separated into communication with one another. This is especially important in the case of young people and adults who are interested in their maturation, such as teachers,

[5] An analysis basic to judgments and moral thinking is found in William G. Cole, *Sex in Christianity and Psychoanalysis* (New York: Oxford University Press, 1955).

[6] An unusually good discussion of sexual semantics is found in a controversial book by Rey Anthony, *The Housewife's Handbook on Selective Promiscuity* (New York: Documentary Books, 1962), Part 2.

parents, youth leaders. Adults also need much experience in free, but probing discussions within their own groups. This would gradually enable them to speak of sex without so much fear or concern of offending. It would help to free our speech of ambiguities and evasions and to develop a vocabulary less laden with anxiety and emotion. Even now the current emphasis on evolving a sexual morality which recognizes cultural developments is forcing our society in the direction of such an interchange.[7] Good communication in regard to sexual matters is obviously an essential. Once the dialogue is under way, semantics will be seen as an essential ingredient in moral development.

The reconciliation of our language with what we actually want to say would be the final, logical step. Full agreement at this level can probably never be attained, but I envision several possibilities. First, some of our language would be freed of the vulgar connotations barring its use. Second, new words and expressions would evolve, as discussion proceeds, to express nuances and subtleties. Third, a broader and a more developmental view of sexuality would demand a vocabulary to support this view.

What we have ahead of us is clearly a long-term, but a challenging task.

7 Lester A. Kirkendall, "Sex and Social Policy," *Clinical Pediatrics.*

Some people tend to talk about sex more openly than others, but everyone communicates about sex in his own way. Use your own discretion about showing this article to your _____. (Fill in the blank: e.g., Mom, Lover, dog, room-mate, etc.)

talking about sex by not talking about sex

Sherri Cavan

Taboos in our society generally prevent us from talking about sex in a direct or explicit fashion. Any other than an indirect approach to sex talk can categorize the speaker as crude, vulgar, and probably over-preoccupied with the subject.

In our society, sex is a very serious matter. Like income and race, it provides one criterion for imputing moral character. We often evaluate people by their choice of sexual objects. If they appear to show no discrimination, we think them licentious. If they prefer their own sex, we deem them queer. If they have what we think are too many sexual encounters, they are promiscuous; if too few, they are prudes. Those who are compulsive in their sexual behavior we regard as attempting to prove their masculinity. We categorize sexual behavior, if money is exchanged, as prostitution. And the presumed proficiency, style, and attitude of the participants, too, reflect on their general moral character. Like other serious matters, we consider sexual topics more properly approached indirectly rather than directly. Just as it is improper to ask someone how much money he makes yearly, so too it is improper to ask people how often they have sexual intercourse, or whether they want it right now.

Because of taboos, sex talk characteristically takes the form of metaphor and innuendo. An analogous situation arises from the Jewish tradition that regards any direct mention of the name of God as an impropriety. Jews therefore have a variety of institutionalized ways of referring to Him so that any good Jew will know when God is being talked about even when His name is never explicitly mentioned.

By using metaphor and innuendo, we are able to imply a great deal more than is being said. It is always possible to talk about sex even when it seems as if we were talking about something else. Similarly, the transition from other topics of conversation to the topic of sex can be smoothly made—sometimes the transition not even being noticed by one participant or the other. Discussion of sex can be expressed in such oblique language that the question may always be asked as to whether the participants are, in fact, even talking about sex at any particular moment. Finally, since sex talk is not carried on with the precision of legal contracts, the extent of our commitment to a proposed or nascent sexual relationship can at any given time remain an open question.

THE TIME AND PLACE

How can we be sure that we are talking about sex? How do we manage to say what we want to say, being aware that any direct mention of the subject would immediately classify the speaker as a boor? For adult members of American society, common sense knowledge of the world includes an understanding of situations where sex talk is or is not likely. By and large, we understand sex talk is more likely to occur in a time and place of leisure activities rather than at work. It is understood that we are more inclined to talk about sex at the movies, the beach, in the park, in bars, at vacation resorts, hotels, ski lodges, and at social parties than in offices, on a bus, in a doctor's waiting room, in the supermarket, or a church. This is not to say that casual sex talk never takes place in the latter situations, but only that a particular kind of finesse is necessary in order that what is taking place can be more or less known by both participants.

Similarly, we generally understand that talk about sex is more likely to take place between conversational participants who see each other as compatible sexual partners. This means that participants of the encounter are much more likely to be talking about sex when they are of opposite sexes, more or less the same age, without obvious marital attachments, and of similar social backgrounds. Again, this is not to say that sex cannot be talked about by those of the same sex, those who are clearly married or engaged to someone else, or those who differ considerably in age or social background. But like talking about sex in unpromising settings or on unpromising occasions, it is not as easy to manage. Given the proper conjunction of setting and participants, however, casual sex talk is not only relatively easy to manage, but quite likely to take place.

FLIRTATION

Casual sex talk is broadly any kind of flirtatious sociability. It may be no more than toying with the notion of seduction and being seduced without seriously expecting that seduction will occur, as in a wink or the protracted, cryptic smile. Or it may lead to actually negotiating a physical sexual encounter—a sociological euphemism for the social euphemism of "making love."

Just as there are socially institutionalized means for knowing when it is likely that one might engage another in casual sex talk, so, too, are there socially institutionalized ways for carrying out such talk. Flirtations may be spontaneously desired by one participant or another, but the way they are carried out tends to make them an almost ritualized formality, much like the *correria* in Latin American countries. There, collective flirtations take place between groups of young men and groups of young women through the ritual means of openly strolling around the plaza. The men proceed in one direction, the women in another, while members of one group are surreptitiously glancing at particular members of the opposite group.

In Rome, "the art of ogling" takes form in many guises, Russell Baker comments:

There are many techniques for the male. One of the most popular is the Bookkeeper's Stare. A woman approaches. The Roman stares into her eyes, then glances rapidly downward from shoulder to calf like a bookkeeper adding a column of figures . . . .

In American society, we find an example of the ritual procedures of casual sex talk by looking at what happens in bars. Bars are commonly understood to be likely places for such activity. In fact, in some bars casual sex talk has a kind of institutional character to it, especially in those places known to be "pick-up" bars. Although professionals such as B-girls and prostitutes engage in rituals for making commercial contacts in bars, by and large casual sex talk rituals tend to be the domain of the nonprofessional; and the rituals of the professionals tend to be attenuated forms of those the nonprofessionals employ. . . .

WHERE THE ACTION IS

Once the participants have located themselves in the appropriate setting, the ritual of casual sex talk in bars ensues. It is a social game in which it is assumed that all patrons there are open to conversation with strangers. Almost anyone present can be considered a likely participant in a known pick-up bar, more so than in bars generally. The patrons of the latter, however, are similarly disposed unless they elect to sit in the booths or at tables away from the bar, a strategy for proclaiming oneself unavailable for participation.

Given a population of possible female co-participants, the male in the bar can instigate casual sex talk either directly or indirectly. A direct opening move would be one where he starts a conversation with a very general remark. "Do you live around here?" or " . . . work around here?" or "The weather has been particularly nice/particularly bad/unusual . . ." Or, "They make the best martinis [Irish coffee, Pim's Cup, etc.] in town here."

An indirect opening requires the assistance of the bartender. This usually takes place when the male is sitting too far from the chosen female to address her directly. The male asks the bartender to "give the lady another of what she's drinking," with the understanding that the bartender will indicate with a nod of his head with whose compliments the drink has arrived. If the woman accepts the drink and conveys her thanks directly to the man with a look and a smile, he may then come over to join her. Once he has joined her in this manner, his opening remarks are almost identical with those which are made when the initial contact is direct, as in "Do you live [work] around here . . . ?"

THE STRUCTURE OF THE RITUAL

When a conversation has been initiated between a man and a woman—once the initial overture and acceptance have been completed—the game moves from casual talk-in-general to casual sex talk. The transformation from *just talk* to *sex talk* characteristically takes place by the participants signifying that the latter is acceptable. This signification is made and acknowledged by means of an exchange of ritual information.

The first such bit of ritual information is that concerning the participants' availability for flirtations. Often statements of availability will be made even before names are exchanged; for if it turns out that neither party is available, there may be no reason for self-introductions. Statements which are read as statements of availability are of the following sort: "This is a hard city for a single person to meet people," or "This is the anniversary of my divorce," or even "Are you alone, too?"

Information about availability is strategic information, as it conveys in part at least what the possible nature of the ensuing conversation will be. If the participants do not declare themselves as available, the conversation may continue; but it will be understood then to be simply casual talk. . . .

MOVIE HOUSE ACTION

The same structural qualities that appear in other flirtations can be seen in the ritual of the movie house encounter. As with pick-up bars, it is a matter of common knowledge among some segments of the population that certain movie houses have more action than others. Thus, casual sexual encounters can take place in any movie house, although some tend to be much more heavily used for this purpose than others—for example, downtown movie houses and those in the vicinity of high schools.

In movie house encounters, it is again up to the male to make the first overture, which, again, as in bars, is characteristically a change in location. Specifically, he moves to the seat directly adjoining that of the female or the one directly behind her. However, the proclamation of the availability to such encounters must be first signified by the female. She sits in the first nine or ten rows of the theater, with an empty seat on at least one side of her if she is with another female, or a seat vacant on both sides of her if she is alone. (Unescorted single females can sit on the aisle without being disturbed.) A female's proclamation of her availability can be further heightened by frequent trips up the aisle, ostensibly motivated by the desire for popcorn or candy. . . .

The characteristic feature of middle-class American society is the routinization of life. It would seem that the ritualization of sex talk is a way of eliminating chance and risk from casual encounters, in favor of clear and precise paths, which, if carefully followed, will lead either to success or at least to failure without loss of face.

Perhaps the proliferation of marriage manuals in our time is likewise an attempt to eliminate risk from sexual encounters. If the mystery is removed, if sex is treated openly and candidly, readers of these manuals are led to believe, they can be assured of efficient performance.[1]

Sexual activity is common to all but the very lowest forms of life. But man's sexual activity is different from the rutting of animals. Because human beings are, as Alfred Korzybski said, a symbolic class of life, man transforms sexual activity from a routine and mundane biological event into an occasion for ritual and ceremony, in the same way that he has managed to transform the routine activity of the linguistic exchange of information into poetry. We can survive without poetry, of course. But the question is, do we really want to?

Were sexual encounters to be treated and transacted with the same explicit candor as checking out a library book or making a bank deposit, there might be nothing left but simple physical gratification, something which can be achieved by one as well as by two.

Sex talk, as it is practiced in our society, with metaphor and innuendo, veiled hints and accepted formal rituals, remains an eminently social activity.

[1] Lionel S. Lewis and Dennis Brisset, "Sex as Work: A Study of Avocational Counseling," Social Problems, XV, 8-18.

KEEP TALKING

All problems are not merely verbal,
The philosophers tell me in uncounted thousands of words—
    but

I tried making love with my mouth taped shut
And I lost my love.

I tried making friends with my mouth taped shut
And I lost my friend.

I tried making war with my mouth taped shut
But no one was angry and the shooting stopped.

I went about the streets with my mouth taped shut
And they took me to the nuthouse

Where I am to this day
Wondering
If all problems are not merely verbal.

Claude Coleman

This article about non-verbal communication first appeared in *Playboy* magazine. I considered putting in the *Playboy* centerfold instead of the article (one "see" is worth a thousand "tells"), but I chickened out. The article is interesting anyway.

THE SOUNDS OF SILENCE

Edward and Mildred Hall

Bob leaves his apartment at 8:15 A.M. and stops at the corner drugstore for breakfast. Before he can speak, the counterman says, "The usual?" Bob nods yes. While he savors his Danish, a fat man pushes onto the adjoining stool and overflows into his space. Bob scowls and the man pulls himself in as much as he can. Bob has sent two messages without speaking a syllable.

Henry has an appointment to meet Arthur at 11 o'clock: he arrives at 11:30. Their conversation is friendly, but Arthur retains a lingering hostility. Henry has unconsciously communicated that he doesn't think the appointment is very important or that Arthur is a person who needs to be treated with respect.

George is talking to Charley's wife at a party. Their conversation is entirely trivial, yet Charley glares at them suspiciously. Their physical proximity and the movements of their eyes reveal that they are powerfully attracted to each other.

José Ybarra and Sir Edmund Jones are at the same party and it is important for them to establish a cordial

52

relationship for business reasons. Each is trying to be warm and friendly, yet they will part with mutual distrust and their business transaction will probably fall through. José, in Latin fashion, moved closer and closer to Sir Edmund as they spoke, and this movement was miscommunicated as pushiness to Sir Edmund, who kept backing away from this intimacy, and this was miscommunicated to José as coldness. The silent languages of Latin and English cultures are more difficult to learn than their spoken languages.

In each of these cases, we see the subtle power of nonverbal communication. The only language used throughout most of the history of humanity (in evolutionary terms, vocal communication is relatively recent), it is the first form of communication you learn. You use this preverbal language, consciously and unconsciously, every day to tell other people how you feel about yourself and them. This language includes your posture, gestures, facial expressions, costume, the way you walk, even your treatment of time and space and all material things. All people communicate on several different levels at the same time but are usually aware of only the verbal dialog and don't realize that they respond to nonverbal messages. But when a person says one thing and really believes something else, the discrepancy between the two can usually be sensed. Nonverbal-communication systems are much less subject to the conscious deception that often occurs in verbal systems. When we find ourselves thinking, "I don't know what it is about him, but he doesn't seem sincere," it's usually this lack of congruity between a person's words and his behavior that makes us anxious and uncomfortable.

Few of us realize how much we all depend on body movement in our conversation or are aware of the hidden rules that govern listening behavior. But we know instantly whether or not the person we're talking to is "tuned in" and we're very sensitive to any breach in listening etiquette. In white middle-class American culture, when someone wants to show he is listening to someone else, he looks either at the other person's face or, specifically, at his eyes, shifting his gaze from one eye to the other.

If you observe a person conversing, you'll notice that he indicates he's listening by nodding his head. He also makes little "Hmmm" noises. If he agrees with what's being said, he may give a vigorous nod. To show pleasure or affirmation, he smiles; if he has some reservations, he looks skeptical by raising an eyebrow or pulling down the corners of his mouth. If a participant wants to terminate the conversation, he may start shifting his body position, stretching his legs, crossing or uncrossing them, bobbing his foot or diverting his gaze from the speaker. The more he fidgets, the more the speaker becomes aware that he has lost his audience. As a last

measure, the listener may look at his watch to indicate the imminent end of the conversation.

Talking and listening are so intricately intertwined that a person cannot do one without the other. Even when one is alone and talking to oneself, there is part of the brain that speaks while another part listens. In all conversations, the listener is positively or negatively reinforcing the speaker all the time. He may even guide the conversation without knowing it, by laughing or frowning or dismissing the argument with a wave of his hand.

The language of the eyes—another age-old way of exchanging feelings—is both subtle and complex. Not only do men and women use their eyes differently but there are class, generation, regional, ethnic and national cultural differences. Americans often complain about the way foreigners stare at people or hold a glance too long. Most Americans look away from someone who is using his eyes in an unfamiliar way because it makes them self-conscious. If a man looks at another man's wife in a certain way, he's asking for trouble, as indicated earlier. But he might not be ill mannered or seeking to challenge the husband. He might be a European in this country who hasn't learned our visual mores. Many American women visiting France or Italy are acutely embarrassed because, for the first time in their lives, men really look at them—their eyes, hair, nose, lips, breasts, hips, legs, thighs, knees, ankles, feet, clothes, hairdo, even their walk. These same women, once they have become used to being looked at, often return to the United States and are overcome with the feeling that "No one ever really looks at me anymore."

Analyzing the mass of data on the eyes, it is possible to sort out at least three ways in which the eyes are used to communicate: dominance *vs.* submission, involvement *vs.* detachment and positive *vs.* negative attitude. In addition, there are three levels of consciousness and control, which can be categorized as follows: (1) conscious use of the eyes to communicate, such as the flirting blink and the intimate nose-wrinkling squint; (2) the very extensive category of unconscious but learned behavior governing where the eyes are directed and when (this unwritten set of rules dictates how and under what circumstances the sexes, as well as people of all status categories, look at each other); and (3) the response of the eye itself, which is completely outside both awareness and control—changes in the cast (the sparkle) of the eye and the pupillary reflex.

The eye is unlike any other organ of the body, for it is an extension of the brain. The unconscious pupillary reflex and the cast of the eye have been known by people of the Middle Eastern origin for years—although most are unaware of their knowledge. Depending on the context, Arabs and others look either directly at the eyes or deeply *into* the eyes of their interlocutor. We became aware of this in the Middle East several years ago while looking at jewelry. The merchant suddenly started to push a particular bracelet at a customer and said, "You buy this one." What interested us was that the bracelet was not the one that had been consciously selected by the purchaser. But the merchant, watching the pupils of the eyes, knew what the purchaser really wanted to buy. Whether he specifically knew *how* he knew is debatable.

A psychologist at the University of Chicago, Eckhard Hess, was the first to conduct systematic studies of the pupillary reflex. His wife remarked one evening, while watching him reading in bed, that he must be very interested in the text because his pupils were dilated. Following up on this, Hess slipped some pictures of nudes into a stack of photographs that he gave to his male assistant. Not looking at the photographs but watching his assistant's pupils, Hess was able to tell precisely when the assistant came to the nudes. In further experiments, Hess retouched the eyes in a photograph of a woman. In one print, he made the pupils small, in another, large; nothing else was changed. Subjects who were given the photographs found the woman with the dilated pupils much more attractive. Any man who has had the experience of seeing a woman look at him as her pupils widen with reflex speed knows that she's flashing him a message.

The eye-sparkle phenomenon frequently turns up in our interviews of couples in love. It's apparently one of the first reliable clues in the other person that love is genuine. To date, there is no scientific data to explain eye sparkle; no investigation of the pupil, the cornea or even the white sclera of the eye shows how the sparkle originates. Yet we all know it when we see it.

One common situation for most people involves the use of the eyes in the street and in public. Although eye behavior follows a definite set of rules, the rules vary according to the place, the needs and feelings of the people, and their ethnic background. For urban whites, once they're within definite recognition distance (16-32 feet for people with average eyesight), there is mutual avoidance of eye contact—unless they want something specific: a pickup, a handout or information of some kind. In the West and in small towns generally, however, people are much more likely to look at and greet one another, even if they're strangers.

It's permissible to look at people if they're beyond recognition distance; but once inside this sacred zone, you can only steal a glance at strangers. You *must* greet friends, however; to fail to do so is insulting. Yet, to stare too fixedly even at them is considered rude and hostile. Of course, all of these rules are variable.

A great many blacks, for example, greet each other in public even if they don't know each other. To blacks, most eye behavior of whites has the effect of giving the impression that they aren't there, but this is due to white avoidance of eye contact with *anyone* in the street.

Another very basic difference between people of different ethnic backgrounds is their sense of territoriality and how they handle space. This is the silent communication, or miscommunication, that caused friction between Mr. Ybarra and Sir Edmund Jones in our earlier example. We know from research that everyone has around himself an invisible bubble of space that contracts and expands depending on several factors: his emotional state, the activity he's performing at the time and his cultural background. This bubble is a kind of mobile territory that he will defend against intrusion. If he is accustomed to close personal distance between himself and others, his bubble will be smaller than that of someone who's accustomed to greater personal distance. People of North European heritage—English, Scandinavian, Swiss and German—tend to avoid contact. Those whose heritage is Italian, French, Spanish, Russian, Latin American or Middle Eastern like close personal contact.

People are very sensitive to any intrusion into their spatial bubble. If someone stands too close to you, your first instinct is to back up. If that's not possible, you lean away and pull yourself in, tensing your muscles. If the intruder doesn't respond to these body signals, you may then try to protect yourself, using a briefcase, umbrella or raincoat. Women—especially when traveling alone—often plant their pocketbook in such a way that no one can get very close to them. As a last resort, you may move to another spot and position yourself behind a desk or a chair that provides screening. Everyone tries to adjust the space around himself in a way that's comfortable for him; most often, he does this unconsciously.

Emotions also have a direct effect on the *size* of a person's territory. When you're angry or under stress, your bubble expands and you require more space. New York psychiatrist Augustus Kinzel found a difference in what he calls Body-Buffer Zones between violent and nonviolent prison inmates. Dr. Kinzel conducted experiments in which each prisoner was placed in the center of a small room and then Dr. Kinzel slowly walked toward him. Nonviolent prisoners allowed him to come quite close, while prisoners with a history of violent behavior couldn't tolerate his proximity and reacted with some vehemence.

Apparently, people under stress experience other people as looming larger and closer than they actually are. Studies of schizophrenic patients have indicated that they sometimes have a distorted perception of space, and several psychiatrists have reported patients who experience their body boundaries as filling up an entire room. For these patients, anyone who comes into the room is actually inside their body, and such an intrusion may trigger a violent outburst.

Unfortunately, there is little detailed information about normal people who live in highly congested urban areas. We do know, of course, that the noise, pollution, dirt, crowding and confusion of our cities induce feelings of stress in most of us, and stress leads to a need for greater space. The man who's packed into a subway, jostled in the street, crowded into an elevator and forced to work all day in a bull pen or in a small office without auditory or visual privacy is going to be very stressed at the end of his day. He needs places that provide relief from constant overstimulation of his nervous system. Stress from over-crowding is cumulative and people can tolerate more crowding early in the day than later; note the increased bad temper during the evening rush hour as compared with the morning melee. Certainly one factor in people's desire to commute by car is the need for privacy and relief from crowding (except, often, from other cars); it may be the only time of the day when nobody can intrude.

In crowded public places, we tense our muscles and hold ourselves stiff, and thereby communicate to others our desire not to intrude on their space and, above all, not to touch them. We also avoid eye contact, and the total effect is that of someone who has "tuned out." Walking along the street, our bubble expands slightly as we move in a stream of strangers, taking care not to bump into them. In the office, at meetings, in restaurants, our bubble keeps changing as it adjusts to the activity at hand.

Most white middle-class Americans use four main distances in their business and social relations: intimate, personal, social and public. Each of these distances has a near and a far phase and is accompanied by changes in the volume of the voice. Intimate distance varies from direct physical contact with another person to a distance of six to eighteen inches and is used for our most private activities—caressing another person or making love. At this distance, you are overwhelmed by sensory inputs from the other person—heat from the body, tactile stimulation from the skin, the fragrance of perfume, even the sound of breathing—all of which literally envelop you. Even at the far phase, you're still within easy touching distance. In general, the use of intimate distance in public between adults is frowned on. It's also much too close for strangers, except under conditions of extreme crowding.

In the second zone—personal distance—the close phase is one and a half to two and a half feet; it's at this distance that wives usually stand from their husbands in public. If another woman moves into this zone, the wife will most likely be disturbed. The far phase—two and a half to four feet—is the distance used to "keep someone at arm's length" and is the most common spacing used by people in conversation.

The third zone—social distance—is employed during business transactions or exchanges with a clerk or repairman. People who work together tend to use close social distance—four to seven feet. This is also the distance for conversations at social gatherings. To stand at this distance from someone who is seated has a dominating effect (e.g., teacher to pupil, boss to secretary). The far phase of the third zone—seven to twelve feet—is where people stand when someone says, "Stand back so I can look at you." This distance lends a formal tone to business or social discourse. In an executive office, the desk serves to keep people at this distance.

The fourth zone—public distance—is used by teachers in classrooms or speakers at public gatherings. At its farthest phase—25 feet and beyond—it is used for important public figures. Violations of this distance can lead to serious complications. During his 1970 U.S. visit, the president of France, Georges Pompidou, was harassed by pickets in Chicago, who were permitted to get within touching distance. Since pickets in France are kept behind barricades a block or more away, the president was outraged by this insult to his person, and President Nixon was obliged to communicate his concern as well as offer his personal apologies.

It is interesting to note how American pitchmen and panhandlers exploit the unwritten, unspoken conventions of eye and distance. Both take advantage of the fact that once explicit eye contact is established, it is rude to look away, because to do so means to brusquely dismiss the other person and his needs. Once having caught the eye of his mark, the panhandler then locks on, not letting go until he moves through the public zone, the social zone, the personal zone and, finally, into the intimate sphere, where people are most vulnerable.

Touch also is an important part of the constant stream of communication that takes place between people. A light touch, a firm touch, a blow, a caress are all communications. In an effort to break down barriers among people, there's been a recent upsurge in group-encounter activities, in which strangers are encouraged to touch one another. In special situations such as these, the rules for not touching are broken with group approval and people gradually lose some of their inhibitions.

Although most people don't realize it, space is perceived and distances are set not by vision alone but with all the senses. Auditory space is perceived with the ears, thermal space with the skin, kinesthetic space with the muscles of the body and olfactory space with the nose. And, once again, it's one's culture that determines how his senses are programmed—which sensory information ranks highest and lowest. The important thing to remember is that culture is very persistent. In this country, we've noted the existence of culture patterns that determine distance between people in the third and fourth generations of some families, despite their prolonged contact with people of very different cultural heritages.

Whenever there is great cultural distance between two people, there are bound to be problems arising from differences in behavior and expectations. An example is the American couple who consulted a psychiatrist about their marital problems. The husband was from New England and had been brought up by reserved parents who taught him to control his emotions and to respect the need for privacy. His wife was from an Italian family and had been brought up in close contact with all the members of her large family, who were extremely warm, volatile and demonstrative.

When the husband came home after a hard day at the office, dragging his feet and longing for peace and quiet, his wife would rush to him and smother him. Clasping his hands, rubbing his brow, crooning over his weary head, she never left him alone. But when the wife was upset or anxious about her day, the husband's response was to withdraw completely and leave her alone. No comforting, no affectionate embrace, no attention—just solitude. The woman became convinced her husband didn't love her and, in desperation, she consulted a psychiatrist. Their problem wasn't basically psychological but cultural.

Why has man developed all these different ways of communicating messages without words? One reason is that people don't like to spell out certain kinds of messages. We prefer to find other ways of showing our feelings. This is especially true in relationships as sensitive as courtship. Men don't like to be rejected and most women don't want to turn a man down bluntly. Instead, we work out subtle ways of encouraging or discouraging each other that save face and avoid confrontations.

How a person handles space in dating others is an obvious and very sensitive indicator of how he or she feels about the other person. On a first date, if a woman sits or stands so close to a man that he is acutely conscious of her physical presence—inside the intimate distance zone—the man usually construes it to mean that she is encouraging him. However, before the man starts moving in on the woman, he should be sure what

message she's really sending; otherwise, he risks bruising his ego. What is close to someone of North European background may be neutral or distant to someone of Italian heritage. Also, women sometimes use space as a way of misleading a man and there are few things that put men off more than women who communicate contradictory messages—such as women who cuddle up and then act insulted when a man takes the next step.

How does a woman communicate interest in a man? In addition to such familiar gambits as smiling at him, she may glance shyly at him, blush and then look away. Or she may give him a real come-on look and move in very close when he approaches. She may touch his arm and ask for a light. As she leans forward to light her cigarette, she may brush him lightly, enveloping him in her perfume. She'll probably continue to smile at him and she may use what ethologists call preening gestures—touching the back of her hair, thrusting her breasts forward, tilting her hips as she stands or crossing her legs if she's seated, perhaps even exposing one thigh or putting a hand on her thigh and stroking it. She may also stroke her wrists as she converses or show the palm of her hand as a way of gaining his attention. Her skin may be unusually flushed or quite pale, her eyes brighter, the pupils larger.

If a man sees a woman whom he wants to attract, he tries to present himself by his posture and stance as someone who is self-assured. He moves briskly and confidently. When he catches the eye of the woman, he may hold her glance a little longer than normal. If he gets an encouraging smile, he'll move in close and engage her in small talk. As they converse, his glance shifts over her face and body. He, too, may make preening gestures—straightening his tie, smoothing his hair or shooting his cuffs.

How do people learn body language? The same way they learn spoken language—by observing and imitating people around them as they're growing up. Little girls imitate their mothers or an older female. Little boys imitate their fathers or a respected uncle or a character on television. In this way, they learn the gender signals appropriate for their sex. Regional, class and ethnic patterns of body behavior are also learned in childhood and persist throughout life.

Such patterns of masculine and feminine body behavior vary widely from one culture to another. In America, for example, women stand with their thighs together. Many walk with their pelvis tipped slightly forward and their upper arms close to their body. When they sit, they cross their legs at the knee or, if they are well past middle age, they may cross their ankles. American men hold their arms away from their body, often swinging them as they walk. They stand with their legs apart (an extreme example is the cowboy, with legs apart and thumbs tucked into his belt). When they sit, they put their feet on the floor with legs apart and, in some parts of the country, they cross their legs by putting one ankle on the other knee.

Leg behavior indicates sex, status and personality. It also indicates whether or not one is at ease or is showing respect or disrespect for the other person. Young Latin-American males avoid crossing their legs. In their world of *machismo,* the preferred position for young males when with one another (if there is no older dominant male present to whom they must show respect) is to sit on the base of their spine with their leg muscles relaxed and their feet wide apart. Their respect position is like our military equivalent: spine straight, heels and ankles together—almost identical to that displayed by properly brought up young women in New England in the early part of this century.

American women who sit with their legs spread apart in the presence of males are *not* normally signaling a come-on—they are simply (and often unconsciously) sitting like men. Middle-class women in the presence of other women to whom they are very close may on occasion throw themselves down on a soft chair or sofa and let themselves go. This is a signal that nothing serious will be taken up. Males, on the other hand, lean back and prop their legs up on the nearest object.

The way we walk, similarly, indicates status, respect, mood and ethnic or cultural affiliation. The many variants of the female walk are too well known to go into here, except to say that a man would have to be blind not to be turned on by the way some women walk—a fact that made Mae West rich before scientists ever studied these matters. To white Americans, some French middle-class males walk in a way that is both humorous and suspect. There is a bounce and looseness to the French walk, as though the parts of the body were somehow unrelated. Jacques Tati, the French movie actor, walks this way; so does the great mime, Marcel Marceau.

Blacks and whites in America—with the exception of middle- and upper-middle-class professionals of both groups—move and walk very differently from each other. To the blacks, whites often seem incredibly stiff, almost mechanical in their movements. Black males, on the other hand, have a looseness and coordination that frequently makes whites a little uneasy; it's too different, too integrated, too alive, too male. Norman Mailer has said that squares walk from the shoulders, like bears, but blacks and hippies walk from the hips, like cats.

All over the world, people walk not only in their own characteristic way but have walks that communicate the nature of their involvement with whatever it is they're doing. The purposeful walk of North Europeans is an important component of proper behavior on the job. Any male who has been in the military knows how essential it is to walk properly (which makes for a continuing source of tension between blacks and whites in the Service). The quick shuffle of servants in the Far East in the old days was a show of respect. On the island of Truk, when we last visited, the inhabitants even had a name for the respectful walk that one used when in the presence of a chief or when walking past a chief's house. The term was *sufan* which meant to be humble and respectful.

The notion that people communicate volumes by their gestures, facial expressions, posture and walk is not new; actors, dancers, writers and psychiatrists have long been aware of it. Only in recent years, however, have scientists begun to make systematic observations of body motions. Ray L. Birdwhistell of the University of Pennsylvania is one of the pioneers in body-motion research and coined the term kinesics to describe this field. He developed an elaborate notation system to record both facial and body movements, using an approach similar to that of the linguist, who studies the basic elements of speech. Birdwhistell and other kinesicists such as Albert Sheflen, Adam Kendon and William Condon take movies of people interacting. They run the film over and over again, often at reduced speed for frame-by-frame analysis, so that they can observe even the slightest body movements not perceptible at normal interaction speeds. These movements are then recorded in notebooks for later analysis.

To appreciate the importance of nonverbal-communication systems, consider the unskilled inner-city black looking for a job. His handling of time and space alone is sufficiently different from the white middle-class pattern to create great misunderstandings on both sides. The black is told to appear for a job interview at a certain time. He arrives late. The white interviewer concludes from his tardy arrival that the black is irresponsible and not really interested in the job. What the interviewer doesn't know is that the black time system (often referred to by blacks as C.P.T.—colored people's time) isn't the same as that of whites. In the words of a black student who had been told to make an appointment to see his professor: "Man, you *must* be putting me on. I never had an appointment in my life."

The black job applicant, having arrived late for his interview, may further antagonize the white interviewer by his posture and his eye behavior. Perhaps he slouches and avoids looking at the interviewer; to him, this is playing it cool. To the interviewer, however, he may well look shifty and sound uninterested. The interviewer has failed to notice the actual signs of interest and eagerness in the black's behavior, such as the subtle shift in the quality of the voice—a gentle and tentative excitement—an almost imperceptible change in the cast of the eyes and a relaxing of the jaw muscles.

Moreover, correct reading of black-white behavior is continually complicated by the fact that both groups are comprised of individuals—some of whom try to accommodate and some of whom make it a point of pride *not* to accommodate. At present, this means that many Americans, when thrown into contact with one another, are in the precarious position of not knowing which pattern applies. Once identified and analyzed, nonverbal-communication systems can be taught, like a foreign language. Without this training, we respond to nonverbal communications in terms of our own culture; we read everyone's behavior as if it were our own, and thus we often misunderstand it.

Several years ago in New York City, there was a program for sending children from predominantly black and Puerto Rican low-income neighborhoods to summer school in a white upper-class neighborhood on the East Side. One morning, a group of young black and Puerto Rican boys raced down the street, shouting and screaming and overturning garbage cans on their way to school. A doorman from an apartment building nearby chased them and cornered one of them inside a building. The boy drew a knife and attacked the doorman. This tragedy would not have occurred if the doorman had been familiar with the behavior of boys from low-income neighborhoods, where such antics are routine and socially acceptable and where pursuit would be expected to invite a violent response.

The language of behavior is extremely complex. Most of us are lucky to have under control one subcultural system—the one that reflects our sex, class, generation and geographic region within the United States. Because of its complexity, efforts to isolate bits of nonverbal communication and generalize from them are in vain; you don't become an instant expert on people's behavior by watching them at cocktail parties. Body language isn't something that's independent of the person, something that can be donned and doffed like a suit of clothes.

Our research and that of our colleagues has shown that, far from being a superficial form of communication that can be consciously manipulated, nonverbal-communication systems are interwoven into the fabric of the personality and, as sociologist Erving Goffman has demonstrated, into society itself. They are the warp and woof of daily interactions with others and they influence how one expresses oneself, how one experiences oneself as a man or a woman.

Nonverbal communications signal to members of your own group what kind of person you are, how you feel about others, how you'll fit into and work in a group, whether you're assured or anxious, the degree to which you feel comfortable with the standards of your own culture, as well as deeply significant feelings about the self, including the state of your own psyche. For most of us, it's difficult to accept the reality of another's behavioral system. And, of course, none of us will ever become fully knowledgeable of the importance of every nonverbal signal. But as long as each of us realizes the power of these signals, this society's diversity can be a source of great strength rather than a further—and subtly powerful—source of division.

SMILES AS COMMUNICATION

Smiles make for pretty faces
and cozy feeling hearts

But also

Salesladies
sorry mothers
guilty toddlers
hesitant lovers
nurses of dying soldiers
unfaithful husbands
pickpockets
Internal Revenue agents
absolute strangers

they all smile

their faces
are dispensaries of smiles

So
it is not
What is a smile
it is
What is in a smile

But will it warm your heart
my smile to you just now
should you question its realness?

Oh come on, baby with hurt knees
come on, beloved stranger
sugar pill or not, take my smile
I want you to be happy
and that is real

Bozena Nemcova

To most of us, this is a pretty familiar scene. So familiar that we may tend to feel that we see more in it than is there for us to see. Try answering the questions below and see how you come out.

Which of the following statements are true, false, or cannot be answered at all?

		(T)	(F)	(?)
1.	The Jones family owns a TV set	( )	( )	( )
2.	Johnny is doing his homework while he watches TV	( )	( )	( )
3.	Johnny's father is a stockholder	( )	( )	( )
4.	The screen is showing a scene from a Western	( )	( )	( )
5.	Mrs. Jones is knitting a sweater	( )	( )	( )
6.	Mr. Jones is a cigar smoker	( )	( )	( )
7.	There are three people in the room	( )	( )	( )
8.	The Jones family subscribes to TIME, LIFE and FORTUNE	( )	( )	( )
9.	The Jones family consists of Mr. Jones, Mrs. Jones and Johnny	( )	( )	( )
10.	They have a cat for a pet	( )	( )	( )
11.	They are watching an evening television show	( )	( )	( )

(Answers on page 62)

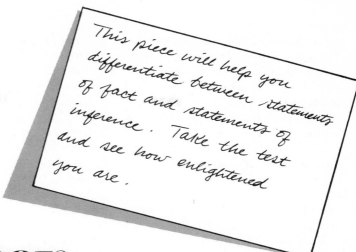

as a matter of fact

Don Fabun

If you played the little game on the opposite page, chances are that you felt that at least some of the statements about the people in the picture were "true." You may have considered them statements of "fact."

And you may have been a little disconcerted to discover that some of the things you called "facts" are what we are going to call "inferences."

Let us see if we can explain what we mean by "fact" and "inference" because everything we have said so far in this issue has been built around what we believe to be the difference between the two. (For instance, the first pages of the book tried to show that "facts" are something that happens inside of us and that everything we say about what happened inside of us is *not* the fact, but is only what we say about it. We can say that something looks like something, but we cannot say what it *"is,"* apart from what it looks—sounds, tastes, feels, etc.–like.)

So, we'll say that a "fact" (for you) is something you personally experienced. And we will go further and say that everything else is an "inference" (for you).

These are harsh definitions. Indeed, if we had to live in a world where there were only "facts" (as we have defined them), it would be a pretty small world, limited to those few things we could personally touch, hear, taste, smell or see. We do not feel that we live in such a world and "common sense" tells us that there are many things we can accept as "facts" that we have not personally experienced.

And we are going to agree with you. We are simply going to say that as long as you are conscious of the difference between "facts" and "inferences" you are less likely to run into trouble when you talk and listen to other people than if you don't distinguish between them.

We can further say that for most common, everyday living a "fact" is something that is socially agreed upon. It can be considered a "fact" if most people believe it to be "true" or if those people who are expert in it agree upon it. We can act *as if* such things were "facts," but we must remember that facts defined in this way are subject to change.

(For example, for a good many centuries most people believed that the world was flat, even though no one actually had reported having seen anyone "fall over the edge." And for several centuries top scientists believed that it was light, shining *out* of your eyes, that made the world visible. Mere consensus does not establish unchanging "facts" because the consensus is based upon what is *said* about an experience).

We may also find it useful to keep in mind that "facts" change with time. Or rather, that facts relate to time. The statements that New York City has a population of 10,000; of 200,000 and of 7,891,000 people were statements of fact *at the time* somebody counted them.

So, perhaps a good way to think about facts is that they are something that happened to you; that they are always historical whenever you try to talk about them. And a good way to think about "inferences" is that they indicate higher or lower probabilities. These probabilities may be high because people have reported them widely and repeatedly. (That the sun will come up tomorrow morning enjoys a very high probability, because in the experience we have had of it, it has always done so. But, as any commuter knows, the fact that the 8:15 train has been on time every morning for the past four days does not mean that it will for sure be on time tomorrow morning. Both statements are inferences; but one has a much higher probability than the other and we can act on that one as if it were a fact).

We can—and do—disagree on "facts" to the extent that our individual experience of the world is different. But what we mostly get into trouble about are disagreements about inferences, which we have stated as if they were facts.

Suppose we both looked through a microscope. We might reasonably agree that that wiggly little thing down there is a wiggly little thing down there. But if I say that is a paramecium, and if you say that it is an amoeba (both statements necessarily inferences) we may be in for an argument.

And we can make this area of disagreement even wider—and thus our chances of understanding each other smaller—if we continue then to make new inferences

concerning the first inference. We can, and sometimes do, build a whole crazy superstructure of inference built on inference—as in the chart on this page concerning the "man with a briefcase."

You can build similar charts around almost any common event in your daily life and quickly discover why you sometimes have difficulty understanding other people—and why, sometimes, they misunderstand you.

NONE OF THE STATEMENTS ON PAGE 60 CAN BE SAID TO BE TRUE FROM WHAT YOU ACTUALLY SAW IN THE PICTURE

1. You do not know that the set is owned by them; it could be borrowed, or a demonstration set.

2. You do not know whether Johnny is doing homework or not; all you can see is that he has a book in front of him.

3. You do not know that Johnny's father is a stockholder; you only know he is looking at the stock market report. Matter of fact, you don't know he is Johnny's father, either. He may be an uncle or friend just visiting in the house.

4. You do not know that it is a Western. It could be a commercial or a foreign-made movie, or almost anything.

5. You do not know that it is Mrs. Jones, and you cannot tell what she is knitting.

DOWN THE YELLOW BRICK ROAD or FROM FACT TO FALLACY

	WHAT HAPPENED	MR. "A" SAYS:		MR. "B" SAYS:	COMMENT
	THE EVENT	"I see a	MAN AND BRIEFCASE	"I see a	No argument
	THE LABEL (1st Inference)	"It is a man with a brief case."	MAN AND BRIEFCASE	"It is a man with a brief case."	Inference because it could be a woman dressed like a man.
	2nd Inference	"He is taking some work home with him."	MAN AND BRIEFCASE	"Spies sometimes use briefcases."	Going off in different directions.
	3rd Inference	"He must be a very dedicated man to take work home with him."	MAN AND BRIEFCASE	"I wouldn't be surprised if that man doesn't turn out to be a spy."	Where's everybody going?
	4th Inference	"A man that dedicated is bound to be a success in life and an asset to our community."	MAN AND BRIEFCASE	"This country is infested with spies and unless we do something about it we're in trouble."	Brother!
	ETC.	ETC.		ETC.	ENDSVILLE

6. You do not know that Mr. Jones (if, indeed, that is Mr. Jones) actually smokes cigars. You only can see that there is a cigar on the ashtray. Perhaps someone else left it there.

7. You do not know how many people might be in the room; you can only see that there are three people in the part of the room shown in the picture.

8. You do not know what magazines they subscribe to. The ones on the table may have been purchased at a newsstand or loaned by a friend.

9. You do not know if this *is* the Jones family; nor can you tell if there are other members of the family who are not present.

10. Could be a neighbor's cat, making itself "at home."

11. You cannot tell if it is evening or not; only that the lights are on. Perhaps it is midday and the shades have been drawn.

communicode 1

Judy L. Haynes

A communicode is a list of communication-related words put into a simple code. The category is given and you can solve the puzzle by thinking of words that belong in the category. The category for this puzzle is "Communication Media," and "Smoke Signals" is an example of a word related to the category. (Smoke Signals is not in code.) To solve the puzzle, try to think of words that begin or end with the same letters or words that have a distinctive pattern of repeated or double letters. If J stands for A in the first word, it will stand for A every time it is used.

If you have difficulty solving the puzzle, a clue is found on page 85. The answer is on page 87.

COMMUNICATION MEDIA

Example: Smoke Signals

Q G W G M R V R L I
Q G W G Y N L I G
Q G W G Z J X Y N
P R W W P L X J U
K R J K H W X J
W G Q Q G J
J X U R L
I G O V Y X Y G J
J G K L J U V
T X Z X S R I G
Y N L Q L Z J X Y N
Y R K Q H J G - Y N L I G

You're undoubtedly an expert practitioner of nonverbal communication, but can you answer questions about it? The questions are on page 87.

SOLUTION FOR COMMUNIQUOTE 1

Shakespeare

There was language in their very gesture.

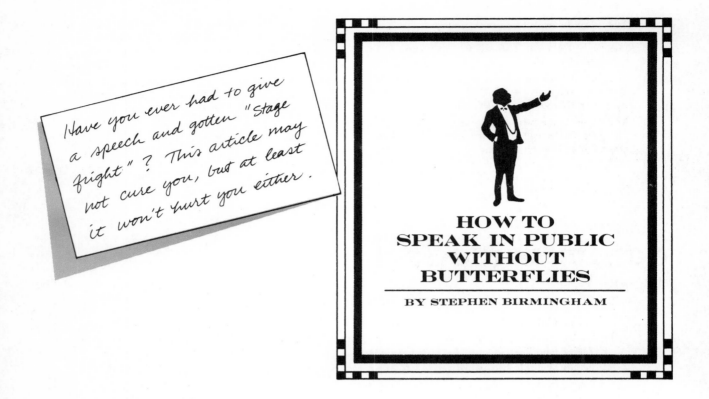

Have you ever had to give a speech and gotten "stage fright"? This article may not cure you, but at least it won't hurt you either.

HOW TO SPEAK IN PUBLIC WITHOUT BUTTERFLIES

BY STEPHEN BIRMINGHAM

My late father, who was a poised and gracious man in most social situations, suffered from a curious phobia. He had an absolute terror of speaking before an audience. It was very strange. As a successful, some even said brilliant, trial lawyer in a medium-sized city, he was professionally most skillful at presenting arguments before a judge and jury in a packed courtroom in behalf of one of his clients. But face him with the prospect of presenting a treasurer's report at a meeting of the local men's club, or ask him to be the master of ceremonies at a testimonial dinner for a friend or business associate, and he was put into a state of jellied panic for weeks beforehand. Perhaps it was because he felt on perfectly safe ground when speaking out in defense of the views or actions of other people. But when required to defend his own position or opinions he was overcome with vast doubts and violent attacks of shyness and insecurity. In any case, he was an adept cross-examiner. As a witness, he would have been hopeless.

HORROR AT HONOR

I remember that once he was invited to be the keynote speaker at a gathering of the American Bar Association in Chicago. It was quite an honor. But the thought of enduring the honor filled him with nothing but horror. He toiled for hours at his desk and in front

of his shaving mirror writing and memorizing his speech, which was expected to last for 30 to 40 minutes. The night before the morning of his address, in an attempt to quiet his jangling nerves and queasy stomach, he stepped into the bar of the Drake Hotel and ordered a stiff Scotch. The one stiff Scotch led to another, and the next led, inevitably, to quite a few more. By the time the Drake bar was ready to close, his partners, who had accompanied him, were able to tell that their chief speaker might well be in serious difficulties by breakfast time. They were right. But, following alternate applications of hot coffee and cold showers, their man was able to make it to the speaker's table virtually unaided. There was a hearty introduction by another lawyer, followed by a round of applause, and the speaker rose and moved to the microphone. As the applause died down, my father suddenly became convinced that the applause was for him, and that he had already delivered his address. Smiling and nodding, he said, "Thank you all very much. Now, are there any questions?" He used to tell the story on himself, with rue.

That story became a joke among my father's legal friends, but sometimes the consequences of this sort of thing can be more serious. The new president of a distinguished New York publishing house was called upon not long ago to deliver a speech before a gathering of his peers. Because he dreaded public speaking, and found his speeches impossible to memorize, he had hit upon the technique of writing out his remarks on a numbered series of large manila cards and reading from them. All went well, on this particular occasion until, about halfway through the speech—and mid-sentence—the speaker flipped over one of his cards and, all at once, the entire stack went cascading to the floor beside him. A kindly soul from the audience stepped forward to help the speaker gather up his cards, but then there remained the problem of reassembling the cards in their proper sequence—a task that only the speaker himself was equipped to do. As he flutteringly shuffled through the suddenly enormous pile of cards, there was utter silence from the speaker's platform. He was literally unable to complete the sentence that he had so manfully begun. As the silence from the lectern drew dreadfully longer, it was accompanied by nervous coughing from the audience. Presently the coughing was supplemented with a giggle here and there. The giggling grew infectious and, at last, the entire audience was dissolved in raucous laughter. Amid the laughter, slapping of thighs and pounding of feet, the speaker—red-faced with humiliation and self-anger—sat down without a single further word.

I confess that I myself have inherited something of my father's affliction and have struggled with it for years. In fact, I feel that the problem may be much more widespread than it appears—so widespread, in fact, that it may be almost universal. Few people, I believe, are born with the ability to present themselves effectively before an audience, or even to get their points across dramatically to a single other human being. Ava Gardner, the actress, has said that she has steadfastly refused to appear in stage plays because of extreme attacks of shyness before large groups. With the relative intimacy of a motion-picture camera, she feels reasonably—though never altogether—comfortable. But she cannot bear the thought of stepping out beneath the proscenium of a real-live theater. As a result, she has turned down a large number of lucrative offers to appear in Broadway plays. Elizabeth Taylor also—who did a stint of Broadway poetry-reading with her husband, Richard Burton—insists that before every performance she was stricken with shattering seizures of what the French call *le trac,* which is just a fancy way of saying stage fright.

A COMMON AGONY

...Hardly anyone is immune to the butterflies—in the beginning, that is. And in today's increasingly competitive society, where hardly anything is offered to any of us without the expectation that we are to deliver something in return, in a society that relies increasingly on the messages in the media of press, radio and television, and in a society where so much is being *sold,* it's become increasingly important that each of us knows how to sell ourselves as best we can. Sometimes, you simply *have* to. You can't just blush bright crimson and sit down in a heap.

As a writer, I was required from early on in my career, to speak at book-and-author lunches, to appear on radio and television talk shows, and to submit to newspaper interviews. I also, to earn a living, had to meet with editors and try to sell my ideas for books and stories, which is exactly like applying for a job, which I have also done. In all of this, I was, of course, not only trying to sell my product—my books and stories—but myself as well.

In the beginning, I was terrible at all of this. Stepping before an audience or microphone, I suffered an instant case of Sahara of the mouth. My words were mouthed with a tongue of cardboard. There was, to be sure, usually a glass of water placed handily within my reach. But I knew that the hand that reached for the glass would tremble so that I could never get it to my lips without spilling water all over my notes. My notes, meanwhile, were of little help because I was also seized with sudden dimness of vision. I could not read them. All was blur. Even worse, of course, was the fact that while I was being terrible I *knew* I was being terrible—and I knew that my audience knew it, and rather pitied me. Clearly, if I was going to continue in this line of work, I was going to have to get better. And over the years I have—if this does not sound too immodest—managed to progress from terrible to not too bad. And so, because they have managed to work for me—and will, I think, work for others on those occasions when they simply have to sell themselves—I will happily pass along a few of the hints and rules I have learned.

DON'T MEMORIZE

If you're asked to make a speech in front of a group, don't try to memorize it ahead of time. Memory, alas, is a faulty instrument at best, and when memory fails before an audience, the results can be disastrous. Mentally sort out and rehearse the points you want to make, and then make them in your own way. Also, memorized speeches come out sounding pat and dull.

Don't write out and *read* your speech, either, for the same reason. If you don't feel confident without notes, make notes, but try to contain them on a single sheet of paper. Remember the catastrophe of the cascading cue-cards. Then, if you have made notes, try not to have to use them. A speech that seems spontaneous and extemporaneous is by far the most effective, and so is a speaker whose eyes never have to travel away from his audience. In mentally organizing your remarks, remember the speechmaker's Rule of Three—that is, first tell your audience what you're going to say, then say it, then tell them that you've said it.

Don't rely on stimulants, alcoholic or otherwise, to help you through the occasion. They'll let you down, as sure as my father's pre-breakfast Scotches did. And don't try to still the butterflies with depressants, either.

Don't be afraid to be natural, to let yourself show through. Don't pontificate, or talk down to your audience. Talk up to them. Don't over-explain what you want to say, but, instead, assume that your listeners have the intelligence to understand your various points as you make them. And, if you suddenly realize that you have forgotten to make a certain point, don't be afraid to interrupt yourself and say, "Oh, by the way, I forgot to mention—." This merely shows your audience that you are fallible and human and makes your audience *like* you.

As you start to speak, look around your audience and pick out the friendly faces, and talk to them. In every group there are always a few that are all smiles and eagerness for what you have to say. They are your blessed allies, and you should make use of them as such. If the sheer physical fact of an audience unnerves you, play mental tricks on yourself. Imagine, for example, that these people are all your dear, close friends, and that you are talking to them in your own living room. Then, when you have familiarized yourself with your audience, be alert for the moment when the faces become less friendly, when the fannies begin to stir uncomfortably in the chairs, or when the audience appears to be looking at its collective wristwatch. That's the moment to start winding it up. There's nothing wrong with leaving a few of your listeners wishing you'd said a little more. They'll like you for that, too.

Learn to recognize—and avoid, any personal mannerisms, facial or vocal, that you may have—nervous throatclearing, for example, or vocalized ("Uh...uh...uh...") pauses between sentences. Buy an inexpensive tape-recorder, talk into it, and then listen to and analyze yourself. Use a mirror and study yourself. Do you grin too much, or gesticulate with your hands too much? This is particularly important in front of a television camera, where hands flying up in front of the picture frame seriously distract the viewer from you and what you are trying to say or sell. President Kennedy discovered that he

had a habit of standing in front of an audience with his hands thrust in his pockets, jangling the keys and coins therein. It was his mother, Rose, who first pointed this out to him, and got him to stand with his hands hanging loosely at the sides, or resting easily on the lectern. It's all right to move about casually as you talk, to scratch your chin occasionally, to shift position slightly, to cross your legs from time to time—anything that makes you seem at ease and natural.

Don't try to be too funny, unless you happen to be Art Buchwald, who can't avoid being funny and gets $5,000 a lecture just for being that way. There's nothing worse than the supposedly funny joke that fails to get a single chuckle. If laughs come, let them, but don't try to force them. And never—under penalty of death or even worse than death—let yourself guffaw loudly at your own jokes.

Learn how to interrupt—forcefully, but also gracefully, without seeming rude. This is particularly important if you are part of a panel or group discussion where you are expected to contribute something, or even if you are in a meeting where your presence is supposed to offer something valuable. A writer friend of mine went on a television talk show and was so overawed by the fame and glamour of the other guests that he never uttered a single word. His purpose on the show—to plug a recent book—was therefore lost entirely. He might as well have not been there. Remember this simple, helpful little motto: Shyness is really just a form of selfishness.

STAY ALERT

Don't just talk—listen, too. Ask questions of your listeners and when they answer, pay sharp attention to what they say. After you talk in public don't be afraid to ask a friend—or a friendly seeming face— "How did I do? Did my talk come off all right? Were they with me, do you think?" Exceptionally helpful hints on your performance and delivery can often come direct from the members of your audience. Listening and not just talking is also important in job interviews. Remember that any company that is considering hiring you is looking for you, or someone like you, to solve some particular corporate problem with your particular talents or abilities. Before you start to sell yourself, find out what that problem is. Then, and only then, come forward and suggest ways in which you, and only you, are exceptionally equipped to solve that problem.

Remember that learning to sell yourself, to present yourself in the best possible light, is like learning to play the piano. It takes practice. It is also a muscular thing, and requires exercise. Exercise and practice your self-selling muscles, and keep them tuned up. Don't cringe away from chances to sell yourself when they are offered. Accept them, and keep accepting them. Even seek them out. The simple fact is that the more you do of it, the better at it you will get to be....

THE BLUE MOVIE: GOODBYE TO ARGYLL SOCKS

This article is about dirty movies. It should be interesting to you regardless of age, race, or dirty movie "track record."

By the way, you should probably rip this article out before you show the book to anyone over thirty.

Maitland Zane

When I was growing up it used to be said that the United States had given the world only one art form. Now there are two: jazz, and the high-class skinflick.

Out of the sewer and into the sunshine of the golden Nixon years—that's the heartwarming, true-to-life saga of America's $500-million-a-year smut industry. It's a story that has everything—romance, drama, raw beauty, power, riches, Women's Liberation, the new sexual freedom, crucial Constitutional questions of censorship and individual freedom, the community's right to protect itself against what the smut smiters call "filth" and "moral pollution" vs. the inalienable right of Americans to read, see, print and talk about anything they damn well want to.

Like jazz music, the blue movie was born in the bawdy house. The first ones were probably cranked off by hand soon after Thomas Alva Edison invented the motion picture camera in 1890, and it is known that stage reels were being shot in the bordellos of Buenos Aires by 1904.[1] By World War I, gentlemen

paid the equivalent of $20 to watch *le cinema bleu* in Paris' best *maisons de tolerance*.

Stag movie-making used to be a fly-by-night business run by the kind of seedy characters you'd expect to find peddling dirty books to schoolboys.

The *ingenues* were embarrassed starlets or smirking, long-in-the-tooth tarts. More often than not, the leading man was a leering little pimp in a pencil moustache and argyll socks—socks and garters he seldom bothered to take off.

Short, blunt, luridly or inadequately lit—and often both funky and funny: those were the stags of yesteryear....

The old-fashioned stags were made for a men-only audience. Women's Lib notwithstanding, I maintain that men's sexuality and turn-ons are different from women's. And always will be. Men are voyeurs, women are exhibitionists. Who has ever heard of a female Peeping Tom? Even the word *voyeuse* sounds preposterous. Men's sport, not women's, that's the way it was during the Argyll Socks Era. With considerable accuracy, considering the prudishness of the times, it was assumed that most women would be offended, if not repelled, by stags. Blue movies were for the Elks' Club, the Legion smoker, the fraternity

[1] The definitive study of the history of the blue movie was a long article by Arthur Knight and Hollis Alpert in the November, 1967, *Playboy*. At least 2,000 films were made between 1920 and 1967, they estimated.

beer party for the pledges, the stag party for the bridegroom the night before the wedding to put him in the proper frame of mind. Reporters in the Forties and Fifties didn't make much money, but they did get to watch fornication on film down at the police station, or at the Federal press room in company with FBI men, assistant U.S. attorneys and sanctimonious Postal Inspectors. "Viewing the evidence," the Postal Inspectors piously called it.

The blue movie was underground, illegal, reprehensible, immoral and fun. As American as cowboy movies, jokes about niggers and Jews, and violence.

Above ground, in "family" theaters, nudity and cusswords were outlawed after some lurid Hollywood scandals of the Twenties and Thirties. Thanks to the blighting hand of the Legion of Decency, the Hays Office and its successor the Johnson Office, even married couples couldn't be seen in bed together. Pajamas and nighties were mandatory, and one of the man's feet had to be on the floor. (It's uncomfortable, but it can be done.)

During the heyday of Joe McCarthyism, a flick called *The Moon Is Blue*, pseudo-titillating and dishonest as any movie ever made, was considered scandalous and given a "Condemned" rating by the Catholic Church. (It made money, lots of money; dirtier money than is now being made by the smut kings, who at least deliver on their promises). Even five years ago it wasn't every American city that permitted bare breasts to be seen on the screen. As for pubic hair and penises...Whew! Theater owners got busted for that.

It's a different world now....

As attitudes change and laws crumble, even society boys and girls are beginning to "model" in skinflicks. And the audiences are changing too. Certain theaters in San Francisco cater to couples, tourist couples, even tour groups of nice Japanese ladies in kimonos, chattering and giggling with their husbands at their sides.

That's progress. Straight housewives going to stag movies and live-sex shows (New York, Los Angeles and San Francisco are among the cities that have them) is a reflection of the psychosexualsocial revolution transforming this country.

The Pill may have begun it all. Now grass is on the way to legality along with pornography. Now it's women's lib and black lib and gay lib. Prudishness and virginity are out, hedonism and sexual freedom are in. In California, where the 21st Century is already beginning, marriage itself is dissolving, often replaced by casual unions, group marriage, bisexual marriage,

"four-marriage," and the swinger-marriage in which suburban mothers may couple with five or ten strangers every Saturday night.

The seventies may go down in history as the Pornographic Decade. Pornography abroad, pornography at home. A revolution boiling up in the cities between the young and old, black and white, the urban poor and the suburban middleclass. Unending, insensate violence in Southeast Asia. And meanwhile, back in Middle America, in respectable theaters in the big cities, millions of people, most of them horny, frustrated middle class white men, spend hundreds of millions of recession dollars to watch the most eyesplitting color movies ever made.

IF IT ISN'T ART, IT MUST BE BUSINESS

Let's look at a typical week's fare in San Francisco's 25-odd hard-core theaters, which cater to 50,000 or more customers a week at between $2.50 and $5 a customer.

In Bob McKnight's Film Festival, which goes in for interracial sex, there's an eerie silence in the audience, while up there on the wide screen a black dude and a pretty white girl (she wearing nothing but nylons and garterbelt) get it all on. A few blocks away in·a sleazy mini-theater in the Tenderloin called the 105 Turk Street Theater, a Danish farmgirl is engaging in fellatio with a 500-pound boar. (*Animal Lover* was the first bestiality movie ever shown openly in San Francisco. The proprietor, one Jackie Simpson, was tried and found guilty of showing an obscene film, and sentenced to six months in jail and a $1250 fine. He is appealing the case.) Across town, in a middle class neighborhood called the Marina, a feature-length sex movie is being shown, with a campy Busby Berkeley-type dance sequence in which several dozen pretty girls dance around singing "You Can't Fuck Around With Love." In a "gay stag" theater called the Nob Hill, six pretty boys mince into a bedroom, undress, and begin a daisy chain. The audience here is sad old queens, one of whom told a man preparing a thesis for his M.A., "I'd give anything to be 30 years younger. I'm sick of being turned down by young men and sleeping with hustlers. I feel like a fool going to these theaters."...

JUST LIKE THE KIDS NEXT DOOR

Skinflick "models," as the euphemism goes, are recruited principally by way of ads in underground papers like the Berkeley Barb, and there's an endless pool of talent. Even the rumor that a skinflick is being shot is enough to have pretty teenage girls lining up around the block, according to Lloyd Downton, who shot several hundred lesbian movies before going to jail for contributing to the delinquency of a minor.

Mary Rexroth, daughter of poet-critic Kenneth Rexroth and herself a bright young poet and actress, has made at least four sex movies, including starring in a pretentious and arty fantasy, *Intersection*, produced by Lowell Pickett.

Twenty-year-old Mary, who looks like a priggish librarian until she takes her glasses and clothes off, came out front and insisted that she really made sex movies for the kicks.

"A lot of chicks claim they're just in it for the money," she said. "But there are a whole lot of easier ways to make money than that. I generally made only $50 a day. The reason I do it—the reason a lot of chicks do it—is because I *enjoy* making films. It's a complete sex trip."

SMUT AND MORALITY: THE RUNNING ARGUMENT

Is smut bad for people? Does watching skinflicks cause crime?

Richard M. Nixon thinks so. Professional smut-smiters like Ray Gauer think so. Conservative psychiatrists like Dr. Louis Noltimier think so, and also do politicians like San Francisco Supervisors Dianne Feinstein and Peter Tamaras. Ditto police and D.A.'s. Few subjects are as violently controversial.

When President Johnson's blue ribbon Commission on Obscenity and Pornography was about to deliver a long and carefully researched report, President Nixon figuratively shot the jury before it got into the jury box.

"The warped and brutal portrayal of sex in books, plays, magazines and movies, if not halted and reversed, could poison the wellsprings of American and Western culture and civilization," the President fumed. He continued: "The pollution of our culture, the pollution of our civilization with smut and filth is as serious a situation as the pollution of our once-pure air and water. Smut should not simply be contained at its present level. It should be outlawed in every state in the Union."

The major findings of the President's Commission—denounced, by the way, by some dissenters led by Nixon's nominee, Charles Keating, a Cincinnati lawyer—were these:

That pornography did not lead to crime or antisocial behavior.

That 60 percent of Americans oppose any controls.

That smut should be kept out of the hands of children, but that otherwise there should be no laws against it so far as adults are concerned, except for controlling offensive advertising.

And that the Commission found "some evidence" that looking at dirty pictures may help some couples achieve a happier sex relationship....

Lieutenant Ray White, who is in charge of sex crimes investigation, claimed that the President's Commission was wrong and that sex movies do produce sex crimes and antisocial behavior.

"Rape attacks are becoming more brutal, bizarre and bestial in character, mirroring the way-out animalism shown in the nearby theaters," White said, discussing the Tenderloin's "adult" moviehouses.

He said that in at least four attacks on women he knew about, the M.O. was the same as depicted in the sex movie then playing.

This opinion varies 180 degrees from some conclusions published in the recent report of the San Francisco Committee on Crime (a 28-member study commission appointed by Mayor Joseph Alioto): "Given the increasingly widespread distribution of pornography in San Francisco over the past year, one would expect to find a corresponding increase in forcible rapes reported to the police if a causal relationship existed between pornography and rape. Yet over the past ten months, forcible rapes reported to the San Francisco police, with ups and downs, have shown a decreasing trend."[2]

Talk to different people and you get diametrically opposite views. The huge majority of American psychologists and psychiatrists, for example, insist that the worst thing that can be said about smut is that it makes men masturbate.

Dr. Martin Blinder, a forensic psychiatrist who has testified for the defense in many obscenity trials, says the voyeur or child molester or rapist or homosexual got that way because of events in his early childhood.

As Dr. Blinder put it, "A man becomes a rapist because he chose the wrong mother, not the wrong movies."

The environment and experiences which turn a person into what society calls a "pervert" or "deviate" occur long before he is ever exposed to explicit sexual materials, Dr. Blinder said.

By adolescence, the sexual pattern is as firmly rooted as if it were "stuck in cement," and virtually nothing can be done to change it without hundreds or thousands of hours of therapy.

Contrariwise, studies show that normal heterosexual adult men are more likely to have been

---

[2] The San Francisco Committee on Crime, *A Report on Non-Victim Crime in San Francisco, Part II: Sexual Conduct, Gambling, Pornography,* June 3, 1971. pp. 68-69.

exposed to pornography than rapists or voyeurs or other persons with sexual maladjustments.

He described the typical "adult" movie patron as a lonely, middleaged, middle-class white man who never has been able to develop a normal sex life.

Dr. Blinder and a Stanford psychologist, Dr. John Davies Black, agreed that for the voyeur, sex films are a "vicarious experience, and in that sense therapeutic."

Although the character of the audiences is changing, as women more and more shake off their protected roles, skinflicks are likely to remain primarily entertainment for the lonely, for stunted individuals who don't want and couldn't handle reality in their sex lives, men who just want to sit there and dream.

So: the potential for an art form exists, but current skinflicks fall woefully short of that potential. "We can't seem to get young people into our theaters no matter how we try," said Les Natali, 30 years old and a man who likes to talk with his pet dachshund in his lap. As far back as 1967 Natali was slipping a few hard-core films, some gay, some straight, into his midnight shows on weekends at the Presidio Theater. And neither he nor any other smut king (or queen) I talked to could really explain why porny movies by and large lay an egg with young people.

"Perhaps they're less uptight, more liberated, more used to 'acting out'," said Natali. "Not just voyeurs, like a lot of our customers."

And from another angle, this further observation of the Committee on Crime cuts through the muddied issues:

> . . . Finally, there is a curious kind of harm that has resulted from the arrest and prosecution of the owners of movie theatres showing pornographic film. . .they have made pornography more important than it should be. Notorious prosecutions have created an aura of intrigue and mystery, and citizens of San Francisco have naturally responded by going to see what the fuss is all about. Just as commercial booksellers have never greeted being "banned in Boston" with great dismay, so too, some commercial theatre owners in the city have been able to depend on a constant supply of headlines manufactured by obscenity prosecutions.
>
> A number of members of the Committee have viewed "pornographic" films at a theatre suggested by the police. Apart from remarking that we found the films extremely bad, we see no need of additional comments, since to do so would simply add to these films an unwarranted dimension of importance. (pp. 76-77)

But the mystery remains. What's erotic to me won't necessarily be erotic to you. What turns on men won't necessarily turn on women. Finally, what's erotic to a "pervert" or "deviate" would probably only make a normal man laugh.

The January, 1971, issue of *Medical Aspects of Human Sexuality* said:

> A study of psychotics and convicted sex offenders found that the picture most frequently selected as pornographic was the famous suntan lotion ad showing the backside of a little girl whose pants were being pulled down by a puppy.

how "white" is your dictionary?

Wm. Walter Duncan

During a recent discussion on semantics in one of my classes, I asked some twenty students to tell me what they think of when the word *white* is mentioned. I got such responses as: "purity," "the color," "snow," "something clean," but not one negative connotation for the word.

I then asked about the word *black* and got: "something very dark," "dirty," "black lies," "death," but not one positive connotation. When I pointed this out to the class, one "white" student immediately exclaimed, "But there are no positive connotations for *black*."

At this point one of the "black" students—all of whom had previously remained silent—responded angrily, and understandably so, pointing out that in his mind there are many negative connotations for *white* and many positive ones for *black*.

After a few moments of tension among some of the students, I turned the discussion into an examination of the word *black,* using the unabridged edition of *The Random House Dictionary of the English Language.* All of the definitions of the word in this dictionary are either negative or neutral in nature. Not until the phrases, specifically item no. 22, *in the black,* does one find a positive connotation for the word, the sole entry in more than fifty lines of fine print that can be said to be of a positive nature. Even when *black clothing* is mentioned, one finds: "esp. as a sign of mourning: *He wore black at the funeral.*"

In contrast with *black, white* has a preponderance of positive meanings, but none with negative connotations—not one word about *white* associated with death, as in *white as a ghost* or with evil, as in *a white mask of deception.*

Now a dictionary is merely a report of the ways words are used. (The precedent set by Samuel Johnson for the expression of personal biases in the definition of some words has long since been rejected by lexicographers.) And the Random House dictionary, in its treatment of the words *white* and *black* is not essentially different from those in other dictionaries. For example, here is the way *Funk & Wagnalls Standard College Dictionary* (Harcourt, Brace & World, 1963) treats the word:

> black adj. 1. Having no brightness or color; Reflecting no light; opposed to *white.* 2. Destitute of light; in total darkness. 3 Gloomy; dismal; forbidding: a *black* future. 4. Having a very dark skin, as a Negro. 5. Soiled; stained. 6. Indicating disgrace or censure: a *black* mark. 7. Angry; threatening: *black* looks. 8. Evil; wicked; malignant: a *black* heart. . .

While all of the dictionaries which I have examined treat the word *black* in a similar manner, the statement that lexicographers merely report the way a word is used, a defense which one editor of a well-known dictionary recently made to me, needs to be examined carefully.

A dictionary is supposedly merely a record of what a language *was* at some point in the past. Even at the moment of publication, a dictionary is dated. No one, therefore, can reasonably expect the dictionaries now in use to have statements about the way the word *black* is currently being used by many people, as in the slogan *black is beautiful,* and only time will tell if *black* is going to become the standard term for *Negro.*

But even if the above arguments are accepted, American dictionaries have not made complete reports of the word *black.* Why, for instance, in listing the phrase *black clothing* were not references made to the formal attire which men sometimes wear to look their best, or to the black robes worn by judges or by academicians? Why weren't references made to the *black opal* or *pearl* or to other contexts in which the word carries a positive connotation?

While a dictionary cannot perhaps explain why a *black lie* is a repugnant case of mendacity and a *white*

an excusable falsehood, a dictionary can suggest that ader compare one phrase with the other. This might many to realize the logical inconsistency of the two phrases and possibly the evil we perpetuate when we use them.

While a dictionary cannot be expected to explain why we call some people "white" and others "black" when in reality there are no black or white people—we are all colored—a dictionary can say "a member of the so-called black race," as *Standard College* does, and a "a member of the so-called white race," as *Standard College* does not.

While a correction and an improvement of the treatment of the words *black* and *white* in our dictionaries may not eliminate prejudice associated with skin color, it could be a contribution to this cause.

rapping in the ghetto

This piece is pretty long, but it has a lot of interesting examples in it. The language may appear "raw," but it represents the real world. (By the way, the article refers to a limited group of ghetto blacks, and the examples should not be generalized to all black people.)

Thomas Kochman

"Rapping," "shucking," "jiving," "running it down," "gripping," "copping a plea," "signifying" and "sounding" are all part of the black ghetto idiom and describe different kinds of talking. Each has its own distinguishing features of form, style, and function; each is influenced by, and influences, the speaker, setting, and audience; and each sheds light on the black perspective and the black condition—on those orienting values and

attitudes that will cause a speaker to speak or perform in his own way within the social context of the black community. . . .

While often used to mean ordinary conversation, rapping is distinctively a fluent and a lively way of talking, always characterized by a high degree of personal style. To one's own group, rapping may be descriptive of an interesting narration, a colorful rundown of some past event. An example of this kind of rap is the answer from a Chicago gang member to a youth worker who asked how his group became organized:

Now I'm goin tell you how the jive really started. I'm goin to tell you how the club got this big. 'Bout 1956 there used to be a time when the Jackson Park show was open and the Stony show was open. Sixty-six street, Jeff, Gene, all of 'em, little bitty dudes, little bitty . . . Gene wasn't with 'em then. Gene was cribbin (living) over here. Jeff, all of 'em, little bitty dudes, you dig? All of us were little.

Sixty-six (the gang on sixty-sixth street), they wouldn't allow us in the Jackson Park show. That was when the parky (?) was headin it. Everybody say, if we want to go the show we go! One day, who was it? Carl Robinson. He went up to the show . . . and Jeff fired on him. He came back and all this was swelled up 'bout yay big, you know. He come back over the the hood (neighborhood). He told (name unclear) and them dudes went up there. That was when mostly all the main sixty-six boys was over here like Bett Riley. All of 'em was over here. People that quit gang-bangin (fighting, especially as a group), Marvell Gates, people like that.

They went on up there, John, Roy and Skeeter went in there. And they start humbuggin (fighting) in there. That's how it all started. Sixty-six found out they couldn't beat us, at *that* time. They couldn't *whup* seven-o. Am I right Leroy? You was cribbin over here then. Am I right? We were dynamite! Used to be a time, you ain't have a passport, Man, you couldn't walk through here. And if didn't nobody know you it was worse than that. . . ."

Rapping to a woman is a colorful way of "asking for some pussy." "One needs to throw a lively rap when he is 'putting the make' on a broad." (John Horton, "Time and Cool People," *Trans*-action, April, 1967.)

According to one informant the woman is usually someone he has just seen or met, looks good, and might be willing to have sexual intercourse with him. My informant says the term would not be descriptive of talk between a couple "who have had a relationship over any length of time." Rapping then, is used at the beginning of a relationship to create a favorable impression and be persuasive at the same time. The man who has the reputation for excelling at this is the pimp, or mack man. Both terms describe a person of considerable status in the street hierarchy, who, by his lively and persuasive rapping ("macking" is also used in this context) has acquired a stable of girls to hustle for him and give him money. For most street men and many teenagers he is the model whom they try to emulate. Thus, within the community you have a pimp walk, pimp style boots and clothes, and perhaps most of all "pimp talk," is a colorful literary example of a telephone rap. One of my informants regards it as extreme, but agrees that it illustrates the language, style and technique of rapping. "Blood" is rapping to an ex-whore named Christine in an effort to trap her into his stable:

Now try to control yourself baby. I'm the tall stud with the dreamy bedroom eyes across the hall in four-twenty. I'm the guy with the pretty towel wrapped around his sexy hips. I got the same hips on now that you X-rayed. Remember that hump of sugar your peepers feasted on?

She said, "Maybe, but you shouldn't call me. I don't want an incident. What do you want? A lady doesn't accept phone calls from strangers."

I said, "A million dollars and a trip to the moon with a bored, trapped, beautiful bitch, you dig? I'm no stranger. I've been popping the elastic on your panties ever since you saw me in the hall. . . .

Rapping between men and women often is competitive and leads to a lively repartee with the women becoming as adept as the men. An example follows:

A man coming from the bathroom forgot to zip his pants. An unescorted party of women kept watching him and laughing among themselves. The man's friends "hip" (inform) him to what's going on. He approaches one woman—"Hey baby, did you see that big black Cadillac with the full tires? ready to roll in action just for you." She answers—"No motherfucker, but I saw a little gray Volkswagen with two flat tires." Everybody laughs. His rap was "capped" (Excelled, topped).

When "whupping the game" on a "trick" or "lame" (trying to get goods or services from someone who looks like he can be swindled), rapping is often descriptive of the highly stylized verbal part of the maneuver. In well-established "con games" the rap is carefully prepared and used with great skill in directing the course of the transaction. An excellent illustration came from an adept hustler who was playing the "murphy" game on a white trick. The "murphy" game is designed to get the *trick* to give his money to the hustler, who in this instance poses as a "steerer" (one who directs or steers customers to a brothel), to keep the whore from stealing it. The hustler then skips with the money.

Look Buddy, I know a fabulous house not more than two blocks away. Brother you ain't never seen more beautiful, freakier broads than are in that house. One of them, the prettiest one, can do more with a swipe than a monkey can with a banana. She's like a rubber doll; she can take a hundred positions.

At this point the sucker is wild to get to this place of pure joy. He entreats the con player to take him there, not just direct him to it.

The "murphy" player will prat him (pretend rejection) to enhance his desire. He will say, "Man, don't be offended, but Aunt Kate, that runs the house don't have nothing but highclass white men coming to her place. . . .You know, doctors, lawyers, big-shot politicians. You look like a clean-cut white man, but you ain't in that league are you? (Iceberg Slim, *Pimp: The Story of My Life)*

After a few more exchanges of the "murphy" dialogue, "the mark is separated from his scratch."

An analysis of rapping indicates a number of things.

For instance, it is revealing that one raps *to* rather than *with* a person, supporting the impression that rapping is to be regarded more as a performance than verbal exchange. As with other performances, rapping projects the personality, physical appearance and style of the performer. In each of the examples given, the intrusive "I" of the speaker was instrumental in contributing to the total impression of the rap.

The combination of personality and style is usually best when "asking for some pussy." It is less when "whupping the game" on someone or "running something down."

In "asking for some pussy" for example, where personality and style might be projected through non-verbal means: stance, clothing, walking, looking, one can speak of a "silent rap." The woman is won here without the use of words, or rather, with words being implied that would generally accompany the non-verbal components.

As a lively way of "running it down" the verbal element consists of personality and style plus information. To someone *reading* my example of the gang member's narration the impression might be that the information would be more influential in directing the listener's response. The youth worker might be expected to say "So that's how the gang got so big," instead of "Man, that gang member is *bad* (strong, brave)" in which instance he would be responding to the personality and style of the rapper. However, if the reader would *listen* to the gang member on tape or could have been present when the gang member spoke he more likely would have reacted more to personality and style, as my informants did.

Remember that in attendance with the youth worker were members of the gang who *already knew* how the gang got started (e.g., "Am I right Leroy? You was cribbin' over here then'") and for whom the information itself would have little interest. Their attention was held by the *way* the information was presented.

The verbal element in "whupping the game" on someone, in the preceding example, was an integral part of an overall deception in which information and personality-style were skillfully manipulated for the purpose of controlling the "trick's" response. But again, greater weight must be given to personality-style. In the "murphy game" for example, it was this element which got the trick to trust the hustler and leave his money with him for "safekeeping."

The funcion of rapping in each of these forms is *expressive*. By this I mean that the speaker raps to project his personality onto the scene or to evoke a generally favorable response. When rapping is used to "ask for some pussy" or to "whup the game" on someone its function is directive. By this I mean that rapping becomes an instrument to manipulate and control people to get them to give up or to do something. The difference between rapping to a "fox" (pretty girl) for the purpose of "getting inside her pants" and rapping to a "lame" to get something from him is operational rather than functional. The latter rap contains a concealed motivation where the former does not.

"Shucking," "shucking it," "shucking and jiving," "S-ing" and "J-ing" or just "jiving," are terms that refer to language behavior practiced by the black when confronting "the Man" (the white man, the establishment, or *any* authority figure), and to another form of language behavior practiced by blacks with each other on the peer group level.

In the South, and later in the North, the black man learned that American society had assigned to him a restrictive role and status. Among whites his behavior had to conform to this imposed station and he was constantly reminded to "keep his place." He learned that it was not acceptable in the presence of white people to show feelings of indignation, frustration, discontent, pride, ambition, or desire; that real feelings had to be concealed behind a mask of innocence, ignorance, childishness, obedience, humility and deference. The terms used by the black to describe the role he played before white folks in the South was "tomming" or "jeffing." Failure to accommodate the white Southerner in this respect was almost certain to invite psychological and often physical brutality. . . .

In the northern cities the black encountered authority figures equivalent to Southern "crackers": policemen, judges, probation officers, truant officers, teachers and "Mr. Charlies" (bosses), and soon learned that the way to get by and avoid difficulty was to shuck. Thus, he learned to accommodate "the Man," to use the total orchestration of speech, intonation, gesture and facial expression for the purpose of producing whatever appearance would be acceptable. It was a technique and ability that was developed from fear, a respect for power, and a will to survive. This type of accommodation is exemplified by the Uncle Tom with his "Yes sir, Mr. Charlie," or "Anything you say, Mr. Charlie."

Through accommodation, many blacks became adept at concealing and controlling their emotions and at assuming a variety of postures. They became competent actors. Many developed a keen perception of what affected, motivated, appeased or satisfied the authority figures with whom they came into contact. Shucking became an effective way for many blacks to stay out of trouble, and for others a useful artifice for avoiding arrest or getting out of trouble when apprehended. Shucking it with a judge, for example, would be to feign repentance in the hope of receiving a lighter or suspended sentence. . . .

Another example of shucking was related to me by a colleague. A black gang member was coming down the stairway from the club room with seven guns on him and encountered some policemen and detectives coming up the same stairs. If they stopped and frisked him he and others would have been arrested. A paraphrase of his shuck follows: "Man, I gotta get away from up there. There's gonna be some trouble and I don't want no part of it." This shuck worked on the minds of the policemen. It anticipated their questions as to why he was leaving the club room, and why he would be in a hurry. He also gave *them* a reason for wanting to get up to the room fast.

It ought to be mentioned at this point that there was not uniform agreement among my informants in characterizing the above examples as shucking. One informant used shucking only in the sense in which it is used among peers, e.g., bullshitting, and characterized the above examples as jiving or whupping game. Others, however, identified the above examples as shucking, and reserved jiving and whupping game for more offensive maneuvers. In fact, one of the apparent features of shucking is that the posture of the black when acting with members of the establishment be a *defensive* one. . . .

The function of shucking and jiving as it refers to blacks and "the Man" is designed to work on the mind and emotions of the authority figure for the purpose of

getting him to feel a certain way or give up something that will be to the other's advantage. . . .

When the maneuvers seem to be *defensive* most of my informants regarded the language behavior as shucking. When the maneuvers were *offensive* my informants tended to regard the behavior as 'whupping the game.' . . .

Shucking, jiving, shucking and jiving, or S-ing and J-ing, when referring to language behavior practiced by blacks, is descriptive of the talk and gestures that are appropriate to "putting someone on" by creating a false impression. The terms seem to cover a range from simply telling a lie, to bullshitting, to subtly playing with someone's mind. An important difference between this form of shucking and that described earlier is that the same talk and gestures that are deceptive to "the Man" are often transparent to those members of one's own group who are able practitioners at shucking themselves. As Robert Conot has pointed out, "The Negro who often fools the white officer by 'shucking it' is much less likely to be successful with another Negro. . . ." Also, S-ing and J-ing within the group has play overtones in which the person being "put on" is aware of the attempts being made and goes along with it for enjoyment or in appreciation of the style.

"Running it down" is the term used by speakers in the ghetto when it is their intention to give information, either by explanation, narrative, or giving advice. In the following literary example, Sweet Mac is "running this Edith broad down" to his friends.

> Edith is the "saved" broad who can't marry out of her religion . . . or do anything else out of her religion for that matter, especially what I wanted her to do. A bogue religion, man! So dig, for the last couple weeks I been quoting the Good Book and all that stuff to her; telling her I am now saved myself, you dig. (Woodie King, Jr., "The Game," *Liberator*, August 1965)

The following citation from Claude Brown uses the term with the additional sense of giving advice:

> If I saw him (Claude's brother) hanging out with cats I knew were weak, who might be using drugs sooner or later, I'd run it down to him.

It seems clear that running it down has simply an informative function, that of telling somebody something that he doesn't already know.

"Gripping" is of fairly recent vintage, used by black high school students in Chicago to refer to the talk and facial expression that accompanies a *partial* loss of face or self-possession, or showing of fear. Its appearance alongside "copping a plea," which refers to a total loss of face, in which one begs one's adversary for mercy, is a significant new perception. In linking it with the street code which acclaims the ability to "look tough and inviolate, fearless, secure, 'cool,' " it suggests that even the slightest weakening of this posture will be held up to ridicule and contempt. There are always contemptuous overtones attached to the use of the term when applied to the others' behavior. One is tempted to link it with the violence and toughness required to survive on the street. The intensity of both seems to be increasing. As one of my informants noted, "Today, you're *lucky* if you end up in the hospital"—that is, are not killed. . . .

The function of gripping and copping a plea is obviously to induce pity or to acknowledge the presence of superior strength. In so doing, one evinces noticeable feelings of fear and insecurity which also result in a loss of status among one's peers.

Signifying is the term used to describe the language behavior that, as Abrahams has defined it, attempts to "imply, goad, beg, boast by indirect verbal or gestural means." (Roger D. Abrahams, *Deep Down in the Jungle*) In Chicago it is also used as a synonym to describe language behavior more generally known as "sounding" elsewhere. . . .

Sounding is the term which is today most widely known for the game of verbal insult known in the past as "Playing the Dozens," "The Dirty Dozens" or just "The Dozens." Other current names for the game have regional distribution: Signifying or "Sigging" (Chicago), Joning (Washington, D.C.), Screaming (Harrisburg), etc. In Chicago, the term "sounding" would be descriptive of the initial remarks which are designed to sound out the other person to see whether he will play the game. The verbal insult is also subdivided, the term "signifying" applying to insults which are hurled directly at the person and the dozens applying to insults hurled at your opponent's family, especially the mother.

Sounding is often catalyzed by signifying remarks referred to earlier such as "Are you going to let him say that about your mama" to spur an exchange between members of the group. It is begun on a relatively low key and built up by verbal exchanges. The game goes like this:

> One insults a member of another's family; others in the group make disapproving sounds to spur on the coming exchange. The one who has been insulted feels at this point that he must reply with a slur on the protagonist's family which is clever enough to defend his honor, (And therefore that of his family). This, of course, leads the other

(once again, more due to pressure from the crowd than actual insult) to make further jabs. This can proceed until everyone is bored with the whole affair, until one hits the other (fairly rare), or until some other subject comes up that interrrupts the proceedings (the usual state of affairs). (Roger D. Abrahams, "Playing the Dozens," *Journal of American Folklore*, July—September, 1962)

. . . An example of the "game" collected by one of my students goes:

Frank looked up and saw Leroy enter the Outpost. Leroy walked past the room where Quinton, "Nap," "Pretty Black," "Cunny," Richard, Haywood, "Bull" and Reese sat playing cards. As Leroy neared the T.V. room, Frank shouted to him.
Frank: "Hey Leroy, your mama—calling you man."
Leroy turned and walked toward the room where the sound came from. He stood in the door and looked at Frank.
Leroy: "Look motherfuckers, I don't play that shit."
Frank (signifying): "Man, I told you cats 'bout that mama jive" (as if he were concerned about how Leroy felt).
Leroy: "That's all right Frank; you don't have to tell these funky motherfuckers nothing; I'll fuck me up somebody yet."
Frank's face lit up as if he were ready to burst his side laughing. "Cunny" became pissed at Leroy.
"Cunny": "Leroy, you stupid bastard, you let Frank make a fool of you. He said that 'bout your mama."
"Pretty Black": "Aw, fat ass head 'Cunny' shut up."
"Cunny": "Ain't that some shit. This black slick head motor flicker got nerve 'nough to call somebody 'fathead.' Boy, you so black, you sweat Permalube Oil."

This eased the tension of the group as they burst into loud laughter.

"Pretty Black": "What 'chu laughing 'bout 'Nap,' with your funky mouth smelling like dog shit."
Even Leroy laughed at this.
"Nap": "Your mama motherfucker."
"Pretty Black": "Your funky mama too."
"Nap:" (strongly) "It takes twelve barrels of water to make a steamboat run; it takes an elephant's dick to make your Grandmammy come; she been elephant fucked, camel fucked and hit side the head with your Grandpappy's nuts."
Reese: "Godorr-dam; go on and rap motherfucker."
Reese began slapping each boy in his hand, giving his positive approval of "Naps" comment. "Pretty Black" in

an effort not to be outdone, but directing his verbal play elsewhere stated:

"Pretty Black": "Reese, what you laughing 'bout? You so square, you shit bricked shit."
Frank: "Whooooowee!"
Reese (sounded back): "Square huh, what about your nappy ass hair before it was stewed; that shit was so bad till, when you went to bed at night, it would leave your head and go on the corner and meddle."
The boys slapped each other in the hand and cracked up.
"Pretty Black": "On the streets meddling, bet Dinky didn't offer me no pussy and I turned it down."
Frank: "Reese scared of pussy."
"Pretty Black": "Hell yeah; the greasy mother rather fuck old ugly, funky cock Sue Willie than get a piece of ass from a decent broad."
Frank: "Godorr-damn! Not Sue Willie."
"Pretty Black": "Yeah ol meat-beating Reese rather screw that cross-eyed, clapsy bitch, who when she cry, tears rip down her ass."
Haywood: "Don't be so mean, Black."
Reese: "Aw shut up, you half-white bastard."
Frank: "Wait man, Haywood ain't gonna hear much more of that half-white shit; he's a brother too."
Reese: "Brother, my black ass; that white ass landlord gotta be this motherfucker's paw."
"Cunny": "Man, you better stop foolin with Haywood; he's turning red."
Haywood: "Fuck yall. (as he withdrew from the "sig" game.)
Frank: "Yeah, fuck yall; let's go to the stick hall."
The group left enroute to the billiard hall. (James Maryland, "Signifying at the Outpost," unpublished term paper for the course *Idiom of the Negro Ghettos*, January 1967.)

The above example of sounding is an excellent illustration of the "game" as played by 15-17-year-old Negro boys, some of whom have already acquired the verbal skill which for them is often the basis for having a high "rep." Ability with words is apparently as highly valued as physical strength. In the sense that the status of one of the participants in the game is diminished if he has to resort to fighting to answer a verbal attack, verbal ability may be even more highly regarded than physical ability.

The relatively high value placed on verbal ability must be clear to most black boys at early age. Most boys begin their activity in sounding by compiling a repertoire of "one liners." When the game is played the one who has the greatest number of such remarks wins. Here are some

examples of "one liners" collected from fifth and sixth grade black boys in Chicago:

Yo mama is so bowlegged, she looks like the bit out of a donut.
Yo mama sent her picture to the lonely hearts club, and they sent it back and said "We ain't that lonely!"
Your family is so poor the rats and roaches eat lunch out.
Your house is so small the roaches walk single file.
I walked in your house and your family was running around the table. I said, "Why you doin that?" Your mama say, "First one drops, we eat."

Real proficiency in the game comes to only a small percentage of those who play it. These players have the special skill in being able to turn around what their opponents have said and attack them with it. Thus, when someone indifferently said "fuck you" to Concho, his retort was immediate and devastating: "Man, you haven't even kissed me yet."

The "best talkers" from this group often become the successful streetcorner, barber shop, and pool hall story tellers who deliver the long, rhymed, witty, narrative stories called "toasts." They are, as Roger D. Abrahams has described, the traditional "men of words" and have become on occasion entertainers as Dick Gregory and Redd Foxx, who are virtuosos at repartee, and preachers, whose verbal power has been traditionally esteemed.

The function of the "dozens" or "sounding" is to borrow status from an opponent through an exercise of verbal power. The opponent feels compelled to regain his status by "sounding" back on the speaker or other group member whom he regards as more vulnerable.

The presence of a group seems to be especially important in controlling the game. First of all, one does not "play" with just anyone since the subject matter is concerned with things that in reality one is quite sensitive about. It is precisely *because* "Pretty Black" has a "Black slick head" that makes him vulnerable to "Cunny's" barb, especially now when the Afro-American "natural" hair style is in vogue. Without the control of the group "sounding" will frequently lead to a fight. This was illustrated by a tragic epilogue concerning Haywood, when Haywood was being "sounded" on in the presence of two girls by his best friend (other members of the group were absent), he refused to tolerate it. He went home, got a rifle, came back and shot and killed his friend. In the classroom from about the fourth grade on fights among black boys invariably are caused by someone "sounding" on the other person's mother. . . .

A summary analysis of the different forms of language behavior which have been discussed above permit the following generalizations:

The prestige norms which influence black speech behavior are those which have been successful in manipulating and controlling people and situations. The function of all of the forms of language behavior discussed above, with the exception of "running it down," was to project personality, assert oneself, or arouse emotion, frequently with the additional purpose of getting the person to give up or do something which will be of some benefit to the speaker. Only running it down has as its primary function to communicate information and often here too, the personality and style of the speaker in the form of rapping is projected along with the information.

The purpose for which language is used suggests that the speaker views the social situations into which he moves as consisting of a series of transactions which require that he be continually ready to take advantage of a person or situation or defend himself against being victimized. He has absorbed what Horton has called "street rationality." As one of Horton's respondents put it: "The good hustler...conditions his mind and must never put his guard too far down, to relax, or he'll be taken." . . .

In conclusion, by blending style and verbal power, through rapping, sounding and running it down, the black in the ghetto establishes his personality; through shucking, gripping and copping a plea, he shows his respect for power; through jiving and signifying he stirs up excitement. With all of the above, he hopes to manipulate and control people and situations to give himself a winning edge.

Whatever Sony hears, is.

A Sony tape recorder answers the riddle.
Still puzzled? See your Sony/Superscope dealer.

SONY SUPERSCOPE

Janice and Abel, the main characters in this story, are both deaf. The story takes place in the mid-1920s and depicts the confusion of a deaf couple in a world of sound. Read on, and as you do, think about the importance of hearing as a communications channel. Do you tend to take it for granted?

In This Sign

Joanne Greenberg

[Janice] was thinking . . . about the mill. There were two other Deaf girls working in the cap room and she hadn't told [Abel]. Half a room away she had seen them, Signing quick and secret over their lunches, and slowly, so no one would look, she had begun to make a way closer to them. It was better to be careful, not to get attention, and three Deaf girls together might bring trouble. So she waited and when the time came, she made Sign, the bare word, fast as thought, a word without breath, without sound, without motion except the flicker seen and known only by people whose lives are turned to motion. They gave her understanding with an eye blink, and at lunchtime, without seeming to move, made a place along the back wall.

They were always together after that, turning no attention to themselves, but sitting by the damp north wall that no one else would choose for an eating place. They sat close, hands hidden by one another's backs, and they talked, leaving only the last minute or two for the crazy eat-without-chewing before the work bell broke them apart. They hated the bell. It came to Janice as a numbing *thrum* up through the bones of her feet and buttocks and up her spine—counting all the hidden ends and edges, the way a blind man must feel things—into the bones of her face; again and again until her

teeth rang and she chewed upon the bell. For Hearing it must be that way always, chewing bells, chewing voices. She wondered how Hearing could stand it—sound. At the bell there was time only for a last swallow, gathering up the greasy papers, brushing crumbs from the lip, the hand-flick good-bye and back to the lighter, smaller chewing of the sound of the roomful of sewing machines.

Janice had been working in the cap room for eight months. Her work was fast. She didn't look at her hands any more; they moved the cloth and took it away without her noticing them. She had found a measuring to her work, regular as a pulse, but faster. After a while it was possible to go for a long time without stopping the machine at all. One hand reached for the new cutout while the other guided the last seams in the cap just finishing under the machine. Now thread came and was fixed with one hand, slowing but not stopping the work and she learned to wind large bobbins tight and full to get more time out of each one. One Saturday she opened her pay envelope and was surprised to find a dollar more in it. It made her frightened. Who was looking for that money, to call her a thief? In the end she had to go to the floor foreman, and he told her the money was "moans," or maybe "pones" or "bones." The fear grew.

She pushed a paper and pencil to the man until he wrote it out; "Bonus—more pay. You go over top quota, you get a *bonus.*"

"Safe money? Good money?"

"Yes."

She took the envelope and walked away, fast, out of the factory and toward home in the freezing almost-dark.

Janice had begun to leave for work early to have a few minutes to laugh and talk with Mary and Barbara before the machines began. When she got to her place that day, Mary was waiting for her, but there was no greeting or gossiping, and the Sign was hard. "You get more money. We know you get bonus-money. Every week." She walked away before Janice had time to answer, and then the bell rang. At lunch break Janice went to where they always sat, but the other girls had already moved farther down and she had to walk the extra way, to mean that she was sorry and wanted to be forgiven. They didn't say anything, but they talk-talked quickly to each other while she sat and ate, her back to the Hearing workroom to protect them. The silence was painful to bear all day and she came home tired and near tears and could not tell Abel why it was. In school she had often done such things to other girls on no more than a whim, and they to her. It was easier in the school where there was always another group to join, new friends, different enemies, wars and truces on a whim. Now a game was everyone, a war, the World. The next day things were the same, and the next after that, and she did not sleep at night. Then the girls got bored with their anger and let her come slowly to the edge of their patience. Afterwards she was slowly forgiven because they needed her and after a week they asked her to show them how she worked.

"My hands aren't fast," she told them, but they didn't want to believe her. She showed them how to use the rhythm of the machine to slow but not stop it while work was opened into it and closed away, changing hands. They raised their eyebrows and made unbelieving faces, but she saw their minds moving toward the ways she had shown them, and the idea of the bonus. When the bell rang, they were eager to get back to their machines. The afternoon passed in its own slowing rhythm and the tiredness of the women thickened the air and pulled back the minutes on the clock. Afternoon air was always bad in the shop. Mary said it was from the lunch boxes of the immigrant girls. Barbara said it was everyone sweating with the windows closed, and they all laughed when Mary said, "That's why the boss walks through in the morning." Sometimes in summer, girls fainted during the afternoon because of the heat and the smell. Janice never told Abel how close she came to being sick with it sometimes. When she complained, he didn't do anything but shrug his shoulders. Anyway, there was a rumor that it was worse in the mill than in the power sewing rooms.

The next day at lunch, Barbara said she had a plan for the three of them. She and Mary had tried Janice's way of working and it speeded the caps through the machine like a miracle. Why not get the quota up, all three of them together, and then go and ask to go into the B Section where the workpants and shirts were made. There, they told Janice, a girl worked on a different rate; faster, for more money. Using the new way, Barbara said, they would be able to do better, since the machines were lighter and faster than the ones they had now for the many thicknesses of the caps. Mary didn't seem as sure as Barbara that a change would help them. Janice said nothing, but decided to herself that she would not go with them. Maybe the new place wouldn't give bonus money and besides, the speed was hers, not theirs. The two of them had taken her speed for their own, as their own idea, and even made big plans on it, when it was hers and not theirs at all. She felt almost too angry to speak to them and her face was hard when the bell rang and they all went back to their machines.

At about four, Janice was working against the heaviness of the air and small flickers of a kind of cramping pain she was beginning to get in her shoulders every day. She felt a hand poking at her back. Sometimes the floor foreman stopped a girl. She took her foot off the petal at the end of a cap and turned to see. It was Mary, and at the other machines the girls were not working and some were standing up, looking toward the other side of the room. They were looking very hard, as if it were more than an interesting thing, as if it were something they needed to see and they would not look away even if someone told them to, or the bell rang. Some of the girls were biting their lips; they were beginning to turn all the way around, watching the main doors. Mary shook a quick B out of her hand—*Barbara*—and Janice stood up and turned too; she got a look of disgust from the girl at the next machine, and she thought it was the first time that the girl had seen her at all. There was someone going out and others were making a big crowd around that spot so the person was not seen. Suddenly the people in the crowd looked as if they were all falling and two of them moved away. Janice saw that the person in the middle was Barbara. People were going with her, walking and also carrying, and before they got her out through the door that the floor foreman was holding open, Janice caught a glimpse of part of the dragging dress that was covered with blood.

"What?" She said it quickly, too frightened to hide the Sign.

"She was going too fast," Mary said. "The machine got her hand."

Janice turned away, feeling sick. She tried to say in her mind that Barbara was only stupid and didn't look what she was doing, but there was her own knowing. Every day some part of looking or thinking went away, stopped and slept and did not follow the cloth or the thread or the rhythm. In front of her stood the same machine, blind and hungry, its silver tooth waiting for the joyful rush downward and the bite of more and more, for a hundred thousand yards of cloth. Every day it ate and ate and pushed across the ticking strips, moving, and if the hand that fed it slipped or was too slow with tiredness, it did not know flesh from cloth. It was just as glad to turn down upon that hand and pull the fingers in and eat them also.

Janice wanted to run away. She looked across the floor. Most of the other girls were back at their machines again and the wheels began to turn as they started up one after another. The floor foreman took three of the girls and they went to get mops and pails and then came back and cleaned up the splattered blood that was on Barbara's machine and trailed out to the aisle and down and out the door. Later he looked over Janice, who was still standing, staring at the door, trembling. He motioned her back to work. Even Mary was at her seat and working again. Janice sat down and began adjusting the stiff cloth under the greedy needle. She knew the other girls were thinking about the blood and the pain and the sick-shock of being hurt, maybe about being crippled and made ugly in their hands. To them hands were only what did ordinary work. In her mind was a picture of hands. It is one of us getting hurt in the hands...one of us. To be without hands...it means to be dumb; it means never to talk again, like to be dead; one of us, without hands . . .

Here is a true story — written for this volume, which demonstrates some problems in intercultural communication. The story also points out that successful communication involves more than good intentions.

BED NEWS

Bernard Gunther

a well-meaning monkey,
seeing a fish in the water
and thinking it was drowning,
took the fish out of the water
and put it on the branch of a tree
to dry

Last winter, I went to Florence to study, and while there I lived in a convent. It was a great deal—no one bothered me, it was extra quiet, and, for all you could eat, it cost only twelve dollars a day.

There at the Villa San Girolamo, where I stayed, I loved my little bed. It was tiny, and the mattress hung over the side, but it was firm, and I loved to lie on it and read. I found it very comfortable, and its vibes were really high.

One morning a disturbing thing happened. Waking up late and hearing the maid outside my door, I thought she wanted to make my bed, so I opened the door and let her in. She asked me something in Italian, and thinking she was asking if she could make the bed, I answered yes. I was still half asleep; I had got into the habit of working most of the night and sleeping very late in the morning with the shutters closed to keep out the morning light. Anyway, the next thing I knew, this guy joined the maid in my room and they began carrying the mattress from my little bed out. I asked, "What are you doing?" but since they answered in Italian, I knew they didn't understand me. For a moment, my foggy mind said, "You're not going to have a bed anymore." I was panicky, because I couldn't communicate with these people. I ran out of my room and next door to the library and found a couple of priests who spoke English, but neither of them spoke Italian. One of them indicated, with no small pride, that he spoke Spanish.

I ran back out into the hall. By this time, the maid and her companion were carrying the bottom of my bed out of my room. I ran down the hall, and this time I found an American priest who did speak Italian. I told him of my plight, and he asked the bed snatchers what they were doing. They said they were going to give me a bigger bed, a better one. This one, they said,

was too small, and because the mattress hung over the sides, it was dangerous. How did they know the new bed would be a better bed? Besides, I didn't think my little bed was too small, or dangerous. I didn't want a "better" bed—I loved the old one!

By this time, they were carrying the monster bed toward my room. The priest shrugged his shoulders and advised, "There's nothing you can do but speak to the Mother Superior." It's like that in Italy; this could happen only in Italy.

I went back to my room where they were putting sheets on the big thing. I felt it; it was soft. I lay down on it; it had bad vibes. It was the wrong size for my room. Everything about the new bed was wrong, and I hated it. I felt unhappy and depressed.

That afternoon, I spoke to the sister in charge of the floor. She explained that she had thought of exchanging the beds because the little one looked uncomfortable, but if I liked, I could have the old one back.

When they moved the little bed back into my room, I was there, with a book, waiting for it. I guess it's still there now, resting where it belongs.

The Fine Art of Complaining

George Weinberg

All of us have something to complain about at some time or another. This piece tells how to make your complaints more effective.

Millions of people choose not to object to what they consider mistreatment, when objecting would greatly improve their lives. Instead, they remain silent, fearing that making a legitimate complaint will reveal a weakness of which the other person will take advantage. Others mistakenly feel that anyone who complains is automatically a troublemaker or a shrew. (These people are usually the children of dominating, haranguing parents, and they'll do anything to avoid being like those parents.)

Others feel that they are worthwhile to other persons only so long as they act compliantly. Nearly all these people think that they have tried to voice their objections and weren't listened to. Usually it turns out that the expressions of dissatisfaction weren't heard, because they were vague or so loaded

with irrelevant insults that the main point was obscured.

In an intimate relationship, when one person suffers as a result of the other's behavior, often the inflicter of pain doesn't realize what he's doing—and may never find out if the sufferer doesn't speak up. Meanwhile, if the sufferer doesn't voice his objection, he predisposes himself to think the worst of the other person—and he may never find out whether the other person *could* control his harmful actions if they were pointed out to him.

Most of us don't want to inflict pain, yet we are all capable of harming the people we love. If a friend or mate belittles you by the way he talks to you or behaves toward you it's your responsibility to tell him, and give him the opportunity to show good faith. But complaining is an art as well as a responsibility, and to make an objection in a way that is fair and forceful and accurate takes practice. The following principles of making and taking criticism, evolved over years of working with college students and married couples, have helped to maintain constructive communication in many relationships.

MAKING CRITICISM

1. *Complain to the person you think is harming you, not to anyone else.*
2. *Try not to object to your mate's behavior in front of someone else.* To most people, being criticized seems like being personally attacked. Your indifference to your mate's comfort, displayed by your willingness to criticize him in front of others, will be taken at least as seriously as the content of what you say. In fairness to him, and for your own sake, wait until you are alone with him.
3. *Don't compare the person's behavior with that of others.* No one wants to be described as inferior to anyone else. Comparisons predispose other people not to listen, even when the complaint is justified. Anyhow, such comparisons always miss the main point.
4. *Make your complaint as soon as you can, when you're alone with the other person and can articulate it.* Speaking up, like any other task, becomes more difficult when you postpone it. Waiting allows your anger to build, and increases the likelihood that you will make irrelevant comments.
5. *Don't repeat a point once you've made it and the other person has carefully considered it.* The reward for patiently listening to criticism ought to be exoneration from having to hear the same crime discussed again.
6. *Object only to actions that the other person can change.* You may ask a person not to shout; but if you ask him not to be angry with you, you're probably expecting too much. I always ask patients who wear sunglasses to take them off in my office, both for their sake and for mine, since I can make better contact with people when I can see their eyes. But though nervousness is often the reason that these people come to my office wearing sunglasses, it would be pointless for me to ask them to relax.
7. *Try to make only one complaint at a time.* If you make more, you'll demoralize the other person and perhaps obscure your major point. For example don't quibble about the carpeting in your office when you've stormed in to ask your boss for a well-deserved promotion. If the subject changes to the price of carpet you'll feel unsatisfied—and your boss may feel he has discharged his obligation by promising to have your carpet changed.
8. *Don't preface your complaint.* "Listen. There's something I've wanted to tell you for a long time. It may hurt you. Please don't feel offended, but..."

   What could be worse? Instead of inoculating your listener against the pain, you are stabbing him to death with your hypodermic needle. By prefaces, you convince both him and yourself that your complaint is to be monstrous, and that probably he won't be capable of receiving it in the same friendly spirit in which you are making it.
9. *After making your complaint in good faith, don't apologize for it.* Apology will only detract from the merit of your accomplishment, in your own mind, and renew your conflict about whether you had the right to say what you did. Apologizing is asking the other person to brace you so you won't fall down under the stress of disagreeing with him. Doing so imposes an unnecessary burden on him.
10. *Avoid sarcasm.* Among sarcasm's invariable motivations are contempt and fear. Your contempt will predispose the other person not to heed you, and because you make a choice not to confront him directly, you intensify your fear of him. Being sarcastic is cowardly and sniveling, no matter how clever the turn of phrase.
11. *Don't talk about other people's motivations when making an objection.* Hardly a man is now alive who doesn't sense the difference between "Please don't interrupt me" and "You never want me to finish what I'm saying."

    "You don't *care* how long I wait for you." "Quit *trying* to make me angry." You give the listener reason to disregard your essential complaint if he concludes that your speculation about his motive is wrong. Steer clear of the tendency to confuse consequence and intention.
12. *Avoid words like "always" and "never."* Exaggerations intended for emphasis when making an objection rob you of accuracy and the psychological advantages that go with it.
13. *If you never compliment the other person, don't expect him to remain open to your criticisms.* Complaints ring loud and long when they're the only sounds that are made. If you want to make occasional objections, you have the obligation to compliment the person at other times. Also, I recommend the practice of thanking people for listening to your criticisms.

TAKING CRITICISM

1. *Be quiet while you are being criticized, and make it clear that you are listening.* Whether you agree or not with what is being said is an issue to be discussed later.

2. *Look directly at the person talking to you.* Only in this way can you convey open reception to what he is saying.

3. *Under no condition find fault with the person who has just criticized you.* If he has made a mistake in grammar, for example, wait a half-hour before telling him. It probably won't seem so important then.

4. *Don't create the impression that the other person is destroying your spirit.* The hardest people to deal with are those who are belligerent at first, and who then, when cornered, act as though they were at the edge of despair. Don't be a fragile bully.

5. *Don't jest.* Flippancy is properly perceived as contemptuous by a great number of people, and is hurtful to just about everyone.

6. *Don't caricature the complaint.* If a person says you were *thoughtless,* don't ascribe to him the statement that you were *vicious* and then defend yourself against a charge he didn't make. The deliberate exaggeration of a charge against you amounts to dismissal of the charge.

7. *Don't change the subject.* Use your intelligence to help articulate the objection, not to obscure it.

8. *Don't imply that your critic has some ulterior, hostile motive.* If you are asking *why* he objected, you are not dealing with his objection. Paraphrasing it is one good way of doing this. In effect, you are saying that you have received the message and noted it.

Don't let people carp at you on the pretext that they're giving you constructive criticism. (You can distinguish carping from criticism by whether the person stays within the rules for making a reasonable objection.) I think you have the right at any time to ask for a short suspension of criticism. Refusal to grant it, or inability to tolerate it, betrays the compulsive critic. The ideal path is narrow: you must be open to criticism but not allow yourself to be tyrannized by it.

SOLVING CLUE FOR COMMUNICODE 1

Q = T; G = E; W = L

Automation and Communication:

a legend

Florence B. Freedman

Not once upon a time, but now; not make-believe, but real: In a clearing of a remote forest, in a country which shall be nameless, stands a completely automated atomic power plant.

So cleverly designed is this plant that the only human needed to tend it is an old watchman whose sole duty is to see that no human enters to interfere with the superbly functioning machinery.

Since even the most cleverly designed machine made by men might conceivably develop a fault, this plant has a device for self-diagnosis and control. If the machinery overheats, it quickly turns itself off; then it dials the phone number of the chief engineer, whose office is in the metropolis. To him it delivers a pre-recorded message: "The machinery has overheated and turned itself off. Please send a repair crew." (If you wonder at the "please," be assured that just because the machine is inhuman, there's no reason for it to be impolite.)

In the life of the atomic power plant it dialed the chief engineer's number three times. Twice the message was received and men were sent to make the necessary repairs. But before the third incident occurred the telephone company, ever alert to improve its system, had made some changes in automatic dialing. This time, instead of reaching the engineer, the message met with this response; "This is a recording. The number you have reached is not a working number. This is a recording. The number you have reached is not..."

Soon after, a soothsayer who lived in the neighborhood forest learned of this in the manner in which soothsayers are wont to acquire information. And he made a notation in his diary:

This is the way the world will end: There will be neither a bang nor a whimper. The only sound or semblance of prayer will be a tape intoning, "The world is ending. The world is ending. Please send a repair crew."

To which the sole reply will be, "This is a recorded message. The number you have reached is not a working number."

signs of approval

Judy L. Haynes

"You did a great job," or "You look really nice tonight," are things that all of us like to hear. The desire for approval has become so widespread throughout our society that certain signs have become associated with approval, such as the "A" on the report card. In the quiz below, your task is to see how many "Signs of Approval" you can identify from the clues. 10 or better is excellent; 7-9 right is good. The answers are on page 115.

AUDIBLE

For a shapely young lady   — — — — — — —

For a speaker   — — — — — — — —

For a touchdown   — — — — —

OBJECTS

For the winner of a tournament   — — — — — —

For a child's paper or forehead (2 words)   — — — —   — — —

For a hero   — — — — —

For a prize-winning bull (2 words)   — — — —   — — — — —

FACIAL—GESTURES

Head movement that says "I agree"   — — —

Facial expression of pleasure   — — — — —

For a job well done, give
yourself a _____ (4 words)   — — —   — —   — — —
     — — — —

Hand sign for approval used
by the Romans (2 words)   — — — — — —   — —

Another communicode is found on page 119. Are you ready to tackle it?

ANSWERS TO COMMUNICODE 1	
Letter	Picture—Phone
Circular	Photograph
Billboard	Magazine
Telegraph	Records
Telephone	Newspaper
Television	Radio

Decisions, Decisions, Decisions

Jay Hall

Group decisions pose special problems. This article presents some information that can help groups reach consensus. Take the test and see how well you score. I blew it!

A disgruntled group member once defined a camel as a horse put together by a committee. Group decisions often are frustrating and inadequate. All members want agreement, but they also want to make their own points heard. So they bargain, they compromise, and the final product is often a potpourri that no group member really believes in. And when group members expect their decisions to be inadequate, they usually are—a self-ful-filling prophecy.

But the group process need not be so ineffective. I have found that when a group's final decision is compared to the independent points of view that the members held before entering the group, the group's effort is almost always an improvement over its average individual resource, and often it is better than even the best individual contribution.

A decision exercise that I developed to illustrate this potential is *Lost On The Moon:* Astronauts have crash-landed on the moon, and their mission is to reach the mother ship 200 miles away. The task is to rank 15 items according to how useful each would be to the lunar mission.

I got experts at National Aeronautics and Space Administration's Crew Equipment Research Department to rank the 15 items for me, with the help of Matthew Radnofsky of NASA's Manned Spacecraft Center in Houston. So there is a correct solution to the *Lost On The Moon* task, or at least a *best* solution.

When individuals take the *Lost On The Moon* test on their own and then meet with three to seven other persons to produce a consensus on the test, the group's decision may be better—closer to NASA's expert opin-ion—than any of the individual decisions had been.

Whether or not this happens depends on the ground rules that the group operates by. I have discovered several rules for group effectiveness in studying the behavior of thousands of small groups.

We were especially pleased to find that many trained groups did better than even their best individual mem-bers. We called this happy event *synergy:* the ability of a group to outperform even its own best individual resource. . . .

I carefully studied several hundred groups to see whether there were typical behaviors that the most effective groups had in common and whether there were interfering strategies that characterized groups that did poorly.

I found that groups that had improved the most and scored the best consistently tried to get every member involved. They actively sought out the points of dis-agreement, and thus promoted conflicts, especially in the early stages. The most ineffective groups, on the other hand, tended to use simple decision techniques, such as majority rule, averaging and bargaining. They seemed to feel a strain toward convergence, as if it were more important to complete the task than to come up with a decision they could all agree on. As one subject in a particularly inept group put it, "the members seemed more committed to reaching a decision than to com-mitting themselves to the decision they reached."

Rules. When I summarized the behaviors of the most effective groups I found I could list all of the apparent decision rules in the form of instructions for group consensus on one typewritten page essentially as fol-lows:

Group-Decision Instructions

Consensus is a decision process for making full use of available resources and for resolving conflicts creatively. Consensus is difficult to reach, so not every ranking will meet with everyone's *complete* approval. Complete unanimity is not the goal—it is rarely achieved. But each individual should be able to accept the group rankings on the basis of logic and feasibility. When all group members feel this way, you have reached consensus as defined here, and the judgment may be entered as a group decision. This means, in effect, that a single person can block the group if he thinks it necessary; at the same time, he should use this option in the best sense of reciprocity.

A Test

Your spaceship has just crash-landed on the moon. You were scheduled to rendezvous with a mother ship 200 miles away on the lighted surface of the moon, but the rough landing has ruined your ship and destroyed all the equipment on board, except for the 15 items listed below.

Your crew's survival depends on reaching the mother ship, so you must choose the most critical items available for the 200-mile trip. Your task is to rank the 15 items in terms of their importance for survival. Place number one by the most important item, number two by the second most important, and so on through number 15, the least important.

_____ Box of matches
_____ Food concentrate
_____ Fifty feet of nylon rope
_____ Parachute silk
_____ Solar-powered portable heating unit
_____ Two .45-caliber pistols

_____ One case of dehydrated milk
_____ Two 100-pound tanks of oxygen
_____ Stellar map (of the moon's constellation)
_____ Self-inflating life raft
_____ Magnetic compass
_____ Five gallons of water
_____ Signal flares
_____ First-aid kit containing injection needles
_____ Solar-powered FM receiver-transmitter

You and four to seven other persons should take this test individually, without knowing each other's answers, then take the test as a group. Share your individual solutions and reach a consensus—one ranking for each of the 15 items that best satisfies all group members. You should read the article, particularly the group-decision instructions on this page, before taking the test as a group.

NASA experts have determined the best solution to this task. Their answers and reasoning are on page 90.

Here are some guidelines to use in achieving consensus.

1. Avoid arguing for your own rankings. Present your position as lucidly and logically as possible, but listen to the other members' reactions and consider them carefully before you press your point.

2. Do not assume that someone must win and someone must lose when discussion reaches a statemate. Instead, look for the next-most-acceptable alternative for all parties.

3. Do not change your mind simply to avoid conflict and to reach agreement and harmony. When agreement seems to come too quickly and easily, be suspicious. Explore the reasons and be sure everyone accepts the solution for basically similar or complementary reasons. Yield only to positions that have objective and logically sound foundations.

4. Avoid conflict-reducing techniques such as majority vote, averages, coin-flips and bargaining. When a dissenting member finally agrees, don't feel that he must be rewarded by having his own way on some later point.

5. Differences of opinion are natural and expected. Seek them out and try to involve everyone in the decision process. Disagreements can help the

LOST ON THE MOON

Items	NASA's Reasoning	NASA's Ranks	Your Ranks	Error Points	Group Ranks	Error Points
Box of matches	No oxygen on moon to sustain flame; virtually worthless	15				
Food concentrate	Efficient means of supplying energy requirements	4				
Fifty feet of nylon rope	Useful in scaling cliffs, tying injured together	6				
Parachute silk	Protection from sun's rays	8				
Solar-powered portable heating unit	Not needed unless on dark side	13				
Two .45 caliber pistols	Possible means of self-propulsion	11				
One case of dehydrated Pet milk	Bulkier duplication of food concentrate	12				
Two 100-pound tanks of oxygen	Most pressing survival need	1				
Stellar map (of the moon's constellation)	Primary means of navigation	3				
Self-inflating life raft	CO_2 bottle in military raft may be used for propulsion	9				
Magnetic compass	Magnetic field on moon is not polarized; worthless for navigation	14				
Five gallons of water	Replacement for tremendous liquid loss on lighted side	2				
Signal flares	Distress signal when mother ship is sighted	10				
First-aid kit containing injection needles	Needles for vitamins, medicines, etc., will fit special aperture in NASA space suits	7				
Solar-powered FM receiver-transmitter	For communication with mother ship; but FM requires line-of-sight transmission and short ranges	5				
			Total _____		_____	

Error points are the absolute difference between your ranks and NASA's (disregard plus or minus signs).

Scoring for individuals:
0-25 = excellent
26-32 = good
33-45 = average
46-55 = fair
56-70 = poor
71-112 = very poor, suggests possible faking or use of earth-bound logic

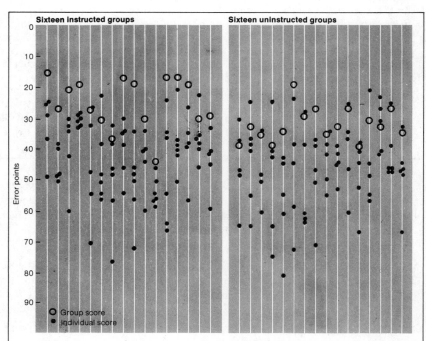

INDIVIDUAL AND GROUP SCORES. Given Group-Decision instructions, 75 per cent of groups did better than their best individuals. Only 25 per cent of uninstructed groups improved on the scores of their best members. Best possible score is 0, worst is 112.

group's decision because with a wide range of information and opinions, there is a greater chance that the group will hit upon more adequate solutions.

Test. These instructions seem to encapsulate the lessons that the trainees had learned in the two-week lab programs. I wondered whether untrained persons could become effective group members by simply reading the list of rules instead of going through the full training program. Fred Watson and I answered this question, using the *Lost On the Moon* exercise with 148 upper-management personnel from several small business organizations. We separated the subjects randomly into 32 discussion groups of four to six members each. They worked on other group activities for about six hours before taking the *Lost On the Moon* test, so in terms of previous experience with each other, the groups were somewhere between the ad-hoc and established groups of our previous studies.

After all subjects had taken the test individually we had 16 of the groups go to their respective group meeting rooms to reach the best decisions they could. We gave the remaining 16 groups the simple instruction sheet and went over it briefly before they went to their meeting rooms.

The instructions were effective. The uninstructed groups, which started with average individual resources of 47.5 error points, produced final decisions averaging about 34 points. But the instructed groups improved significantly more—from 45 points as individuals to 26 points as groups.

Success. The most important factor that determined how well a group performed was the success of its unique judgments—those instances in which the group abandoned existing resources in favor of a new solution that they created for themselves. Both types of groups produced unique judgments on 27 per cent of their decisions. But the instructed groups created qualitatively better solutions than the uninstructed groups did. Thus, the uninstructed groups responded to internal conflict with compromises, which may have eased group tensions, but did not improve the group's decisions. Instructed groups, on the other hand, used conflict to their advantage as an opportunity for creativity.

Most of the instructed groups achieved synergy—75 per cent produced group decisions that surpassed even the best individual decisions. Only 25 per cent of the uninstructed groups did this.

Up. We reached two major conclusions from these studies: (1) that groups function as their members make them function, and (2) that conflict, effectively managed, is a necessary precondition for creativity. Thus, when they follow a few brief instructions, decision-making groups can be expected to do better than even their best members, at least on multiple-judgment tasks of the sort we have studied. There is nothing in the group process that makes committees, boards and panels inherently inept.

Ludicrous, ineffective solutions to problems are the product of groups that are pessimistic about their own potential, and have imperfect ways of dealing with conflict.

The horse that is put together by a committee that understands group dynamics won't turn out to be a camel: it may be a thoroughbred filly fit for the Triple Crown.

How to Sabotage a Meeting

Alfred Fleishman

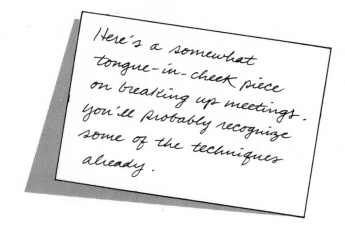

Here's a somewhat tongue-in-cheek piece on breaking up meetings. You'll probably recognize some of the techniques already.

Lots of people talk about "communication" as if they know what they're talking about. They don't.

These people usually know more about how to sabotage communication than they do about how to promote it.

Of course, we're all would-be saboteurs. Most of the time, we do this unconsciously; and since sabotage is a risky business, sometimes we do succeed in communicating in spite of ourselves, having inadvertently stumbled upon some principle of general semantics—like the notion that the words we use may have a different meaning to the person we're talking to than they do to us, even though we both read the dictionary—diligently.

But there are some people around who have really studied the art of sabotage. They like to attend large gatherings ostensibly devoted to the practice of serious discourse—any meeting will do. Meetings offer them the perfect opportunity to be disruptive. The serious student is advised to study their methods.

If you adhere to the following seven rules, and apply them judiciously, you, too, can be an expert at semantic sabotage.

INTERRUPTION

The secret of breaking up any meeting by using the interruption method lies in your timing.

Let the speaker talk just long enough for you to get a general idea of what he's trying to say. Before he has a chance to conclude, interrupt. Arrange it so that you supply the clincher to *his* argument before he can get a word in edgewise. Even if you don't agree with his point of view, it isn't difficult to twist his words to support whatever different point of view you may be advocating at the moment. Of course, the speaker may insist on plodding on. Let him. This not only gives you a chance to interrupt him again, but, by

demonstrating how patient and tolerant you are, wins *you* the support of the audience.

DIVERSION

The diversion technique begins where the interruption technique leaves off. Changing the subject is the best method of diversion, and the easiest for the beginner to follow. The only thing to remember is CHANGE THE SUBJECT COMPLETELY. You can talk about anything—the latest space shot, civil rights, the "good old days"—just so you change the subject completely.

There are, however, more sophisticated ways of creating a diversion. For instance: if several persons are engaged in a seminar, start talking in semi-hushed tones to the person sitting next to you. Put your hand in front of your mouth to make it even more obvious that you are carrying on a separate conversation. This may earn you some dirty looks, but the main thing is that people's attention is being diverted away from the speaker.

There are a few special techniques to cultivate if you use this device. It is important to be able to pitch your voice at a low enough level so as not to drown out the speaker completely. Yet you must create a "buzz." This takes some practice, but it's worth trying. People will attempt to listen to both you and the speaker. They won't be able to. Their heads will begin to turn and their minds to wander away from what the speaker is trying to say. You've won!

NAME CALLING

Name calling is a more advanced technique. Here, you don't interrupt, you wouldn't dream of creating a diversion. You are completely and totally cooperative. BUT, when the speaker has completed his address or succeeded in making his point, call him a name. It's as simple as that. The name should, of course, cast doubt on his character, or on his ability as a thinker. Suggest that he must be "off his rocker" or "out of his mind." Imply that nobody with a grain of sense could say such things or hold such views.

It isn't necessary to use foul language in your implementation of this technique. In fact, it's better if you keep your remarks "clean," because the effectiveness of this device hinges upon loudness and self-confidence. You want to make sure everybody hears what you are saying, and you want to sound extremely sure of yourself. Only as a last resort should you make a statement such as "I don't want to discuss that woman we both know." The distraught speaker will insist on knowing "what woman." All you have to do now is keep repeating that you don't want to embarrass anybody by going into details. This ploy is practically infallible. People being what they are, many of them will be very interested indeed in knowing all about "that woman." But *you* haven't said anything. Can you help it if other people have "dirty" minds?

CHALLENGING THE SPEAKER'S INTEGRITY

To make this particular method of sabotage work, you must permit the speaker to finish what he has to say—however much it hurts. Your aim is to disarm him. Never raise your voice; for you must appear to be in complete agreement with him. Then pounce:

"Who's *really* making the money out of this?"

"What are you trying to hide?"

"What's in this for you?"

"Why aren't all the facts being brought out in the open?" (You can allow yourself a great deal of moral indignation here.)

This will put the speaker on the defensive all right!

CONTRADICTION

You shouldn't have any difficulty with this technique. All you have to do is sit back, wait until the speaker is finished, and then contradict him. Don't attempt to engage him in debate. Just say authoritatively: "You're wrong."

The speaker will probably try to defend his position. Don't pay any attention to him. Simply shrug your shoulders and repeat your original remark. (He's dead wrong, and you know it.) Never make the fatal mistake of actually arguing with him. And whatever you do, don't let him trap you with specifics.

LAUGHING IF OFF

As demonstrated in the interruption technique, one good way to deflate a speaker is by showing his audience how tolerant you are—by laughing him and his subject off.

Remember, it's within your power to turn any discussion into a farce. Of *course*, you'll stay and listen to what the speaker has to say—patiently and with good-natured amusement. But really, you imply, the whole thing is so ridiculous that if you weren't such a "good Joe," you'd get up and walk out right now.

THE BRUSH-OFF

The brush-off is often used ineffectively. The student should be thoroughly versed in the other techniques before he tries this one. Only the real expert can successfully maneuver a speaker away from the podium by opening his briefcase and starting to rearrange its contents.

The beginner often makes the mistake of thinking that he can employ the same tactics to disrupt a meeting as he uses to get rid of an unwanted guest or client. In a public situation, he can't pick up the phone, dial the golf pro at the Country Club, and ask if he can have a quick lesson. That would not only be impractical, but openly rude. The saboteur has to play by the rules, even if he is playing a different game.

No, if you're a beginner, your best bet is to carry the interruption technique to the point of absurdity. Your first attempts will certainly result in chaos—not necessarily semantic chaos, but chaos nonetheless—and you will have achieved your goal. Cut off communication quick!

The comic strips are everyone's favorite part of the newspaper. This article gives the inside story on some of our favorite funnies.

THE FASCINATING FUNNIES

Fred Dickenson

It all started in 1896, when cartoons featuring "The Yellow Kid"—a flap-eared, bald little monster who hit youthful enemies with a golf club and wore what appeared to be a yellow nightgown on which snappy sayings were lettered (the first time that words had been placed *within* a drawing)—began appearing in Joseph Pulitzer's New York *World.* Readers took to The Kid, and soon rival publisher William Randolph Hearst lured his creator, Richard Felton Outcault, away from Pulitzer to draw for his New York *Journal.*

From that moment, comic strips blossomed. Outcault dreamed up Buster Brown, a more refined Kid, and mothers made a whole generation of little boys wear bangs and large collars in imitation. And today, openly or covertly, an estimated 200 million fans follow the fortunes of their favorite characters in some 460 strips and panels published in 3300 newspapers in 150 countries. Blondie tells Dagwood to get off the sofa and mow that lawn in 33 languages and dialects, including Chinese, Icelandic, Afrikaans and Urdu; Mickey Mouse woos Minnie in pidgin English in Lae, New Guinea; Snoopy, the flying beagle of "Peanuts," talks to himself in fluent Greek as well as Arabic. And, in celebration of the 75th anniversary of what has now been hailed as a native art form, a traveling "Cavalcade of American Comics," visiting a score of cities, depicts highlights of the heady rise from Happy Hooligan rags to Daddy Warbucks riches.

It was in 1897 that the longest continuously published strip—"The Katzenjammer Kids," still appearing—rose from the inkwell of Rudolph Dirks. Then came

"Happy Hooligan," who wore a tin can for a hat, conceived by Frederick Burr Opper. And then Opper's "Alphonse and Gaston," those incredibly polite Frenchmen who spent most of their time bowing and saying, "After you . . ."

The public adored them and clamored for more. Warmly lovable or absolutely mad (and often both) characters leaped from the pens of cartoonists to meet the demand. Augustus Mutt, a tall, chinless (and broke) horseplayer created by Harry Conway (Bud) Fisher in 1907, visited a sanitarium and met a pleasant little inmate who thought he was boxing-great James J. Jeffries. Mutt called him Jeff, and a comic legend was born. Ignatz, a mouse with deadly aim directed by George Herriman, began bouncing bricks off the head of a love-smitten "kat" named Krazy. Jiggs, an incorrigible lover of corned beef and cabbage, was the brainchild of George McManus in 1913. Almost 60 years later, Jiggs is still at it in "Bringing Up Father."

Gradually, "Pow!" and "Zowie!"—accompanied by the soles of feet flying out of the last panel—gave way to more gentle humor as artists appreciated the public's growing sophistication. Soon Rube Goldberg could sketch his series, "Foolish Questions," in one of which a bruised man sitting beside a wrecked car is asked, "Have an accident?" His reply: "No, thanks; just had one."

The comics took an even more important turn when Frank King began to draw "Gasoline Alley." In 1921, when Gasoline Alley's Walt Wallet found a baby on his doorstep and named him Skeezix, readers, captivated by the human-interest approach, quickly turned each day to see what was happening to the baby. Skeezix became the first comic-strip character to grow up on the funny pages.

Successful, too, was high adventure, when Harold R. Foster began to illustrate the "Tarzan of the Apes" stories. Later, Foster added to adventure-appeal with his own beautifully drawn and accurately written strip entitled "Prince Valiant."

Today, few areas of pen-and-ink entertainment remain unexplored by the comics. Detectives Rip Kirby, Dick Tracy and Kerry Drake fight crime; Steve Canyon, Buz Sawyer, Superman and Terry Lee (of "Terry and the Pirates") battle evil wherever they find it; Flash Gordon and Buck Rogers probe outer space beyond the dreams of astronauts.

What makes a comic-strip character successful? Nobody knows. Today three of the most popular strips, based on the number of newspapers in which they appear, are: "Blondie," about a scatterbrained wife and her beleaguered husband Dagwood; "Beetle Bailey," the world's laziest soldier; and "Peanuts," featuring a lively group of youngsters and a dog whose fantasies include being a World War I aviator.

"I stick to three basic ideas," says Murat (Chic) Young, whose "Blondie" has been running for 41 years and appears in 1653 newspapers. "They're eating, sleeping and raising a family. Readers all over the world are able to identify with those activities."

However, that does not explain "Beetle," "Peanuts" and hundreds of others; nor do comics fans themselves offer a better clue. Recent surveys made by a major research firm show college-educated executives and husky hardhats following the adventures of a favorite character with equal fervor. Breakdown of readers' ages lists comics fans as 60 percent adults (18 years and older); 15 percent teen-agers (12 to 17); and 25 percent under 12.

Yet, so gossamer is the magic spell of the funnies that some of today's most popular strips almost didn't survive their birth. When "Peanuts" was six months old in 1950, the strip was carried by only a few newspapers and earned Charles Schulz a meager $90 a month. A former newspaperman recalls that at that time he stopped the editor of "Peanuts' " major New York City outlet on an impulse and mentioned that he liked the new feature. "I'm glad you told me," the editor said, "because I'm on my way to a meeting where we're going to discuss dropping it." The timely boost saved the day, and the rest is history. "Peanuts" now appears in more than 1400 newspspers, according to United Feature Syndicate, and grosses something like $20 million a year in miscellaneous royalties.

Avant-garde in many respects, the funnies have had a profound influence in popularizing certain foods and slang expressions. Who hasn't heard of Dagwood sandwiches, Popeye's spinach and Wimpy's hamburgers? And if you think a "goon" was originally a strong-arm bruiser and a "jeep" a jouncy Army vehicle, you're wrong. The goon was a strange, huge "thing" in "Thimble Theatre" that helped the cruel Sea Hag in her endless battles with Popeye and the jeep was a lovable little animal in the same strip that ate orchids, could foretell the future, and said, of all things, "Jeep!"

Appreciating the reach and power of the funnies, the government and organizations devoted to various worthy causes often have called upon them for help. Comics heroes leaped into combat during World War II, and a Sunday-page talk given by Col. Flip Corkin of "Terry and the Pirates" to Lt. Terry Lee about the importance of teamwork in the Air Force was considered worthy of insertion in the *Congressional Record*. Today, comic strips do everything from fighting pollution to promoting the use of zip codes.

Aficionados are vociferous about their likes and dislikes. When "Smitty's" father was killed off in the strip of that name, readers made such a fuss that artist Walter Berndt had to bring him back alive, a victim of "amnesia." After Milt Caniff disposed of pretty Raven Sherman in "Steve Canyon," hundreds of protesting students at Loyola University in Chicago held a memorial service. And an elevator operator in New York, seeing Caniff enter his car, snarled at the artist, "You murderer!"

Nobody seems to mind that time moves or stands still in the funnies according to the whim of the creator. Little Orphan Annie hasn't aged a day in 47 years, but Skeezix has grown to manhood since he was found on Uncle Walt's doorstep, and now has children of his own. It has taken Blondie's tots 30-odd years to become teen-agers.

Where do the funnies go from here? Observers note that, true to their talent for moving with the times, the comics are giving blacks such as Lieutenant Flap in "Beetle" more important roles, and a new strip, "Dateline: Danger!" has two reporters, one white and one black. Two other strips now feature blacks: "Friday Foster" and "Luther." Sophisticated humor in the tradition of "B.C." and "The Wizard of Id" consistently wins enthusiastic new fans.

Certainly, those who turn to the comics each day with an anticipatory smile and a sigh of relief after the usually grim news, seem to hope that the familiar friends who live there will carry on forever. Gluyas Williams' suburbanites, Clare ("When a Feller Needs a Friend") Briggs' embarrassed boys, and H.T. Webster's "Casper Milquetoast" have vanished into the past, but new intimates from the inkwell, thank goodness, are constantly springing to life.

Doonesbury
by GB Trudeau.

CLEAR ONLY IF KNOWN

Edgar Dale

This piece discusses the problems we face in giving and following directions.

For years I have puzzled over the poor communication of simple directions, especially those given me when traveling by car. I ask such seemingly easy question as: Where do I turn off Route 30 for the bypass around the business district? How do I get to the planetarium? Or, is this the way to the university? The individual whom I hail for directions either replies, "I'm a stranger here myself," or gives me in kindly fashion the directions I request. He finishes by saying pleasantly, "You can't miss it."

But about half the time you do miss it. You turn at High Street instead of Ohio Street. It was six blocks to the turn, not seven. Many persons tell you to turn right when they mean left. You carefully count the indicated five stoplights before the turn and discover that your guide meant that blinkers should be counted as stoplights. Some of the directions turn out to be inaccurate. Your guide himself didn't know how to get there.

Education is always a problem of getting our bearings, of developing orientation, of discovering in what direction to go and how to get there. An inquiry into the problem of giving and receiving directions may help us discover something important about the educational process itself. Why do people give directions poorly and sometimes follow excellent directions inadequately?

First of all, people who give directions do not always understand the complexity of what they are communicating. They think it a simple matter to get to the Hayden Planetarium because it is simple for them. When someone says, "You can't miss it," he really means, "I can't miss it." He is suffering from what has been called the COIK fallacy—Clear Only If Known. It's easy to get to the place you are inquiring about if you already know how to get there.

We all suffer from the COIK fallacy. For example, during a World Series game a recording was made of a conversation between a rabid baseball fan and an Englishman seeing a baseball game for the first time.

The Englishman asked, "What is a pitcher?"

"He's the man down there pitching the ball to the catcher."

"But," said the Englishman, "all of the players pitch the ball and all of them catch the ball. There aren't just two persons who pitch and catch."

Later the Englishman asked, "How many strikes do you get before you are out?"

The baseball fan said, "Three."

"But," replied the Englishman, "that man struck at the ball five times before he was out."

These directions about baseball, when give to the uninitiated, are clear only if known. They are, in short, COIK.

Try the experiment sometime of handing a person a coat and asking him to explain how to put it on. He must assume that you have lived in the tropics, have never seen a coat worn or put on, and that he is to tell you verbally how to do it. For example, he may say, "Pick it up by the collar." This you cannot do, since you do not know what a *collar* is. He may tell you to put your arm in the sleeve or to button up the coat. But you can't follow these directions because you have no previous experience with either a sleeve or a button. He knows the subject-matter but he doesn't know how to teach it. He assumes that because it is clear to him it can easily be made clear to someone else.

The communication of teachers and pupils suffer from this COIK fallacy.... A teacher once presented a group of parents of first-grade children with material from a first-grade reader which she had written out in shorthand, and asked them to read it. It was a frustrating experience. But these parents no longer thought it was such a simple matter to learn how to read. Reading, of course, is easy if you already know how to do it....

In giving directions it is easy to overestimate the experience of our questioner. It is hard indeed for a Philadelphian to understand that anyone doesn't

100

know where the City Hall is. Certainly if you go down Broad Street, you can't miss it. We know where it is: why doesn't our questioner? Some major highways are poorly marked. In transferring to Route 128 in Massachusetts from Route 1 you must choose between signs marked "North Shore" and "South Shore." In short, you must be from Boston to understand them...

Another frequent reason for failure in the communication of directions is that explanations are more technical than necessary. Thus a plumber once wrote to a research bureau pointing out that he had used hydrochloric acid to clean out sewer pipes and inquired whether there was any possible harm. The first written reply was as follows: "The efficacy of hydrochloric acid is indisputable, but the corrosive residue is incompatible with metallic permanence." The plumber then thanked them for this information approving his procedure. The dismayed research bureau wrote again, saying, "We cannot assume responsibility for the production of toxic and noxious residue with hydrochloric acid and suggest you use an alternative procedure." Once more the plumber thanked them for their approval. Finally, the bureau, worried about the New York sewers, called in a third scientist who wrote: "Don't use hydrochloric acid. It eats hell out of the pipes."

We are surprised to discover that many college freshmen do not know such words as *accrue, acquiesce, enigma, epitome, harbinger, hierarchy, lucrative, pernicious, fallacious,* and *coerce.* The average college senior does not know such words as *ingenuous, indigenous, venal, venial, vitiate, adumbrate, interment, vapid, accouterments, desultory.* These words aren't hard—if you already know them.

Some words are not understood; others are misunderstood. For example, a woman said that the doctor told her that she had "very close veins." A patient was puzzled as to how she could take two pills three times a day. A parent objected to her boy being called a scurvy elephant. He was called a disturbing element. A little boy ended the Pledge of Allegiance calling for liver, tea, and just fish for all.

Another difficulty in communicating directions lies in the unwillingness of a person to say that he doesn't know. Someone drives up and asks you where Oxford Road is. You realize that Oxford Road is somewhere in the vicinity and feel a sense of guilt about not even knowing the streets in your own town. So you tend to give poor directions instead of admitting that you don't know.

Sometimes we use the wrong medium for communicating our directions. We make them entirely verbal, and the person is thus required to hold them in mind until he has followed out each step in the directions. Think, for example, how hard it is to remember Hanford 6-7249 long enough to dial it after looking it up. A crudely drawn map will often make our directions clear...

But we must not put too much of the blame for inadequate directions on those who give them. Sometimes the persons who ask for help are also at fault. Communication, we must remember, is a two-way process.

Sometimes an individual doesn't understand directions but thinks he does. Only when he has lost his way does he realize that he wasn't careful enough to make sure that he really did understand. How often we let a speaker or instructor get by with such terms as "cognitive dissonance," "viable economy," "parameter," without asking the questions which might clear them up for us. Even apparently simple terms like "needs," "individual instruction," or "interests" hide many confusions. Our desire not to appear dumb, to be presumed "in the know," prevents us from understanding what has been said. Sometimes, too, the user of the term may not know what he is talking about.

We are often in too much of a hurry when we ask for directions. Like many tourists, we want to get to our destination quickly so that we can hurry back home. We don't bother to savor the trip or the scenery. So we impatiently rush off before our informant has really had time to catch his breath and make sure that we understand.

Similarly, we hurry through school and college subjects, getting a bird's-eye view of everything and a close-up of nothing. We aim to cover the ground when we should be uncovering it, probing for what is underneath the surface...

We must neither overestimate nor underestimate the knowledge of the inquiring traveler. We must avoid the COIK fallacy and realize that many of our communications are clear only if already known.

And the whole earth was of one language, and of one speech.

And they said, Go to, let us build us a city and a tower, whose top may reach unto heaven; and let us make us a name, lest we be scattered abroad upon the face of the whole earth.

And the LORD said, Behold, the people is one, and they have all one language; and this they begin to do: and now nothing will be restrained from them, which they have imagined to do.

Go to, let us go down, and there confound their language, that they may not understand one another's speech.

So the LORD scattered them abroad from thence upon the face of all the earth: and they left off to build the city.

Genesis 11:1, 4, 6—8

Did you ever stop to think about the problems to be overcome in producing a lightshow?

LIGHTSHOW

HERE'S MUSIC IN YOUR EYES:

Richard Blystone

FILLMORE East, Camelot of rock music New York Sattidy night. The GRATEful DEAD with FLYing HAIR with TWO guiTARS eLECtric BASS play HEAD-to-HEAD and MAKE THE MIDNIGHT AIR MUD-THICK WITH S-O-U-N-D.

Behind them on a 20-by-30 foot translucent vinyl screen giant pearls bounce to the beat on a field of black velvet. Still farther behind is guru-bearded Ken Richman, perched on a narrow backwall balcony with four overhead projectors, 10 slide projectors, two movie projec-

tors, racks of assorted equipment, a large supply of Cokes, five companions, and an electric dishwasher.

Ken watches the stage on closed-circuit television and hears the rock harden, he pulls his headset back from one ear and moves over to Bill Schwarzbach who looks like young Thomas Jefferson with long hair tied in the back and they confer in the silence of overwhelming NOISE

and Bill reaches into the rack behind him and pulls out a plastic squirt bottle the kind they use for mustard in diners labeled Dark Red Oil and he squirts it into a pool of yellow water in a clock crystal on his overhead projector and a voluptuous swirl of red seeps across the screen behind the Dead and

Cecily Hoyt in long dark hair and green Fillmore East football shirt on the next overhead spins her plate of clear oil and india ink and the pearls wheel in formation and on the next overhead Jane Rixmann in long hair and maroon shirt prepares a shimmy dish by pouring bright blue and red glycerine in a dish over a sun template and holds a dish of clear water in the LIGHT beam

and lean Tom Shoesmith squats on another balcony above in front of a projector and color wheel with bits of mirror on a rubber pad bending LIGHT with his hands and sends spinning nebulae of silver and green across the screen

and the troupe watch intently what they are making; they will never see it just that way again

and the drums come on and the beat gets harder and Ken fires a strobe LIGHT like artillery over the horizon and Bill and Jane and Cecily shake their clock faces and the whole screen EXPLODES with tides and torrents and pinwheelsbobsblotchesspraysspurtsredorangeyellowblueshapesbeyond
WORDS

rotatingthrobbingthrashingspinningdancing GROWING shrinking allatonce and the kidsintheaudience LOSE
their egos in the sublime excess and sit narcotized with hardly a head nod or a foot stomp and
HOLD
the arms of their seats and suddenly it is all over.

A still slide of flowers appears on the blackened screen, and on their balconies in the smell of hot lights the show crew draws a breath.

Midnight is still early for Ken, 19, the "mixer" of the troupe, a combination of quarterback and moderator. And for Bill, 28, and Tom, 27, and Cecily and Jane, both 23, and Joshua White, 27, the founder and leader, who has since left the group to begin experimental work in closed-circuit television.

The late show may go on until nearly dawn, calling on their full repertory of smoke drifts, sunstorms, rainstorms, jelly-bean storms, hairy jewels, jigging petunias, bursting galaxies, and every other cosmic metaphor you can think of. Plus gag slides with words (AWOPBOBALOOBOP ALOPBAMBOOM) or pictures (an ancient shot of Frank Sinatra with floppy bow tie).

In the show's third year as permanent attraction and accompaniment for music at the Fillmore, the terminology for techniques is pretty well standardized although their application is not.

The "blow plate," for example. It employs a film of colored oil floating on a puddle of water in the clock glass. Air from a portable hair dryer directed at one point starts a tidal swirl across the screen.

A squirt of water from a window cleaner bottle, a spin of the plate, a change of focus or of lens, a reflecting wheel or a color wheel, and infinite modifications are possible.

One of the troupe's most memorable effects, the "fast plate," invokes not the cosmic but the microscopic. Put oil of one color and water of another between two clock glasses and squish rhythmically on the projector. On the screen a giant amoeba jounces its vacuoles and flails its pseudopods in a frug of agitation.

"It's a very environmental thing," Tom Shoesmith says. "We've gone from chamber music to music that vibrates your chair. That's very much just tie-in with the louder civilization. So we've gone to a louder visual environment, too."

"What's going on here is that you're playing with the limits of perception: you can crank the volume up until it's almost painful and you can cut it back down until people really have to strain their ears to hear it; you can take the light levels so low that people are really starting to have their information break up between the eye and the brain because the eye shifts to its night-vision thing, and then you can crank the light levels way up again . . ."

Tom, like Bill a Columbia University engineering student before the lure of the theater took over, has a technical-sounding term for it: "sensory overload." There's a simpler one: It's a drugless way of blowing your mind.

"It's just a textbook extension of the American life style and technology in art," Bill says. "It could not be more inevitable, more mainstream, right at the center of the whole forthcoming life style that's causing so much furor."

Bill is from Seattle and somehow looks clean-cut in long hair, goatee, chambray shirt, and bell bottoms.

"The essence of these media events is that the old regulations, the old categories are abolished," he says, "and you re-evaluate and make new rules, new categories."

When you have seven tons of transformers, buttons, switches, projectors, lenses, slides, templates, reflectors, and bottles of dyed water, glycerine, and two weights of mineral oil to cope with, that makes for a lot of rules and categories.

"It's getting to the point now where we can make music ourselves with the lights."

"A lot of times the rock groups will actually get into the light show," Ken adds. "They'll turn around and watch the screen and relate to the screen. And then it becomes a cycle of them watching the screen, getting something, doing musical reaction to the light show reacting to them."

"There's nobody who's seen enough of it yet to offer us a critique," Bill says. "We aren't really artists yet, but we deal with art successfully on our level, you might say, so what does that make us—artisans? I don't know."

Besides the unfathomed complexity of the medium, they say, the chief thing keeping it from being art is lack of money. The troupe is busy taking care of $20,000 worth of temperamental gear and a new refinement often means a big investment.

"It's sort of like being an architect in the Middle Ages going from town to town looking for somebody who's got enough money to put up a cathedral," Tom says.

Touch is probably the most primitive and necessary form of communication. Why do we try to pretend that we don't need or enjoy it?

The Loving Message in a Touch

Norman M. Lobsenz

Not long ago, a couple went to a marriage counselor with a problem. The wife objected violently to being touched. Although she freely enjoyed her sexual relationship with her husband, she could not, to his bewilderment and hurt, bear the affectionate caresses he liked to give her hand or arm or hair.

Another family, concerned about a teen-age son's rebelliousness, consulted a psychiatrist who spent weeks trying to restore communication between the emotionally estranged boy and his father. One day, the father suddenly got up and embraced his son. The boy hugged back, and both began to cry. "It's the first time you've held me since I was a child," the boy said.

These incidents are not as unusual as they may seem. Whether we can admit it or not, many of us are painfully inhibited about touching and being touched even by those we love.

Reasons are not hard to find. The average American tends to think of bodily contact in terms of sex or combat—both of which are prickly with cultural and psychological taboos. Our Puritan heritage leads many of us to disapprove of any touching as "sensual."

Those who have created this invisible barrier have lost something important: the part touch plays in giving encouragement, expressing tenderness, showing emotional support. Touch is a crucial aspect of all human

104

relationships. Yet, except in moments of extreme crisis, we often forget how to ask for—or to offer—this boon. We forget, for instance, how it can heal the wounds of a quarrel. I was told about a mother who tried reasoning with two daughters, 11 and 12, who were fighting bitterly over clothes for a party. When reasoning failed, their annoyed father *ordered* them to be quiet. But it wasn't until the mother impulsively flung her arms about both girls and held them close that the bickering stopped.

We also tend to forget how comforting physical contact can be when we are under stress. When my wife was seriously ill I spent hours in the hospital simply holding her hands—a gesture that was wonderfully sustaining for both of us. Yet, in the ordinary run of life, it seems that even the most loving couples seldom link hands—either in times of sorrow and anxiety, or in moments of peace and pleasure.

An instinctive awareness of the power of touch to convey deep feeling is reflected in such expressions as having a "touching" experience, being "touched" and keeping "in touch." When "words fail," we reach out physically. Helen Keller—blind and deaf from birth—wrote in her diary: "My dog was rolling in the grass. I wanted to catch a picture of him in my fingers, and I touched him lightly. Lo, his fat body revolved, stiffened and solidified into an upright position. He pressed close to me as if to crowd himself into my hand. He loved it with his tail, his paw, his tongue. If he could speak, I believe he would say with me that paradise is attained by touch."

Studies of infants and children have shown repeatedly that nothing is more important to early physical and mental growth than touching. In various experiments with normal and subnormal youngsters, those who had the most physical contact with parents or nurses or attendants learned to walk and talk the earliest and had the higher I.Q.s.

Research with animals yields similar results. In a famous experiment a decade ago, psychologist Harry F. Harlow built two "surrogate" mothers for monkey babies. One, a mother-figure built of wire, gave milk. The other, built of sponge rubber and terry cloth, gave no milk. Given a choice, the baby monkeys went to the terry-cloth mother for the comfort of her soft "touch." These results contradicted the accepted theory that a baby loves its mother primarily because she provides food.

Despite what science, instinct and common sense tell us, many Americans seem to cut down—almost deliberately—on the amount and quality of physical contact. After infancy, words replace touches; distance replaces closeness. With toddlers, touch is used to guard and control children, but less often to play with or show affection to them.

The warning is drummed into them: "Don't touch!" Touching is "not nice." Moreover, care is often taken to make sure that youngsters don't see even their own parents touching each other affectionately. And many parents, who confuse the sexual touch with the tender, caring, restorative or sympathetic touch, are either afraid or ashamed to make physical contact with growing sons and daughters. Little wonder, then, that so many of us learn to do without touching or being touched.

Where does one begin? How does an undemonstrative person learn to touch? Here are suggestions—and cautions—gathered from psychologists who have taken an interest in the matter:

Discuss the idea with your family first. "Don't just suddenly and singly become a 'toucher,'" says psychiatrist Dr. Alexander Lowen. "Nothing is more upsetting than an unexpected and unexplained change in another person's behavior."

Begin by performing simple acts of physical contact that are customary in some, but far from all, families: kissing good night or good morning; hugging when greeting or saying farewell.

Learn to discern when others are in a mood to be touched; otherwise physical contact can be irritating. Children often go through stages of rejecting a parent's touch.

Be emotionally honest when you do touch. Dr. Nicholas Dellis, a New York psychologist, told me that once, when he was extremely busy, his daughter came to him seeking attention. "I put my arm around her, but my mind was on my own problems. She sensed at once that I was not emotionally with her. She said, 'You're holding me *away* from you.' I looked, and the arm I had around her shoulder actually was forcing her apart from me rather than bringing us together."

Try to make the act of touch a source of comfort and reassurance, rather than a veiled demand. Touch should never be a vehicle for clinging to or possessing another person.

Realize that touching does not always have a sexual connotation. Many of us have failed to learn that different kinds of touching, meaning different things, are possible.

Dr. Herbert A. Otto, a pioneer in the search for ways to foster personal growth and expand human potential, believes that much more takes place through touch than most of us realize. It can, he says, almost magically dissolve barriers between people. It can break down the emotional walls we build within ourselves. "Touch," says Dr. Otto, "is always an exchange, if not a sharing. Through touch we grow, and we enable others to grow."

These games may be played in encounter groups or simply with friends. They can change your personality and your life. They are also fun!

games for building warmth and trust

Howard R. Lewis and Harold S. Streitfeld

You can play many of these interpersonal games with just one other person, a friend or your spouse. But these games are derived from *group* experiences and for greatest benefit are best played by three or more. With a number of participants you can build on a broader foundation of perspective, ability and sensitivity and, therefore, can have a richer experience. The foundation is also likely to be more stable—the group setting tends to have a maturing influence on its members, often a welcome safeguard.

On the other hand, the more is not necessarily the merrier. The maximum size for an effective group ranges around a dozen members. For a good rule of thumb, if you have more than fourteen participants present, break up into two groups. . . .

There is at least one . . . ingredient essential to a rewarding group experience: You need to provide a conducive setting. Thus, in bringing together an encounter group, what preparations should you make? Emily Coleman, a lecturer and writer on behavioral sciences, has sponsored parties centered on growth games and offers these tips:

1. *Do ahead of time* whatever you can do to keep things flowing smoothly, without interruptions. Make any snacks beforehand. Put the cat out. Take the phone off the hook. Then relax. "Your mood can't guarantee the success of a party. But if it is bad, others will pick it up, and the whole thing will flop."

2. *Don't invite people who work together* or who are in the same line of business or who know each other really well. "If you do, it will be like fighting City Hall, you against an entrenched organization determined to maintain the status quo. They will talk shop or tell stories or exchange miseries or one-up or do whatever they usually do."

Do invite people in relatively the same socioeconomic level, people you think have something in common, such as interests, goals and values, people who are relatively open minded and people who do not have sandpaper personalities. Keep your guest list small for your maiden effort.

3. *Prepare your guests for a different kind of evening.* Encourage them to ask questions of one another. Give them specific permission to refuse to answer questions that they don't want to answer. Tell them what your plans are for later.

4. *Avoid alcohol if possible.* Otherwise serve only wine or punch. "Be very stingy with liquor if you want these games to be taken seriously and not to be laughed away as nonsense by those persons who are most in need of getting close to people. The persons most alienated from others, most desperately in need of personal contact, may be convinced that they can't function in public without alcohol."

One other pointer: *Keep your first games simple* and devoted to breaking the ice. An excellent way of beginning is to have everyone let out a mighty roar and bang and stamp the floor. People bring a lot of tensions and frustrations to a group, and this is a good way to get them out.

Here is an assortment of other introductory activities:

Getting Acquainted

My Name Is. Perhaps the method most often used to get a group acquainted is to have each member give the name he wishes to be known by and tell what he wants to get out of his experience with the group: resolve an inhibition; get rid of feelings of guilt or resentment; experience closeness.

Now I Feel. Tell the others how you feel sitting here *now*. If you have a special feeling toward any other members—favorable or unfavorable—express it.

Stay in the present moment—"Now I feel tense"; "Now I feel happy." Don't say, "Now I feel that I am tense"; "Now I feel that I am happy." "I feel," as used in this verbal construction, means "I am of the opinion." It is a thought—a conclusion about your observing yourself—and not a genuine tuning-in to your emotions. What do you *feel*?

Values. To break a group into subgroups for quick getting-to-know-you interactions, Dr. Daniel I. Malamud has tried reading off a set of three statements reflecting values of one kind or another. Each member decides which one of the statements he considers most important. The participants are then divided into smaller groups according to their choices.

For example, the items might be: "To be generous toward other people." "To be my own boss." "To have understanding friends." All those who choose "To be generous toward other people" as most important gather together in one subgroup to talk over their choices for five minutes. Another set Malamud has used is: "To have a good meal with a friend." "To get a good night's sleep." "To have a good orgasm."

Birth Order is another Malamud game for getting acquainted. He groups members according to who were the oldest children in their families, who were the youngest, who were the middles. These subgoups go on to explore the various experiences they had by virtue of their birth-order positions.

Conversations

Gibberish. Break up into pairs, and have a nonsense conversation, using only gibberish. As your conversation proceeds, you are likely to find that you can convey a great deal of emotional content without needing words. Can you express affection? Anger? Fear? Joy?

Gibberish can serve another purpose as an icebreaker: It is impossible to be uptight when you and others around you are being absurd. Ergo, to break the ice,

engage in an absurd conversation. One suggestion: Stick your tongue out, and try to talk seriously. You can't be very formal with someone after you've stuck your tongue out at him.

Also fun: Roar. Squeak. Gurgle. Burble. Make other noises. Let your partner imitate yours, then you imitate him. You'll find conversations like this taking place:

"Grnggzblltt."

"Grngbllzt?"

(Insistently) "Grnggzblltt!"

"Ah! Grnggzblltt."

Baffling Conversation can give you an insight into the frustrations of trying to communicate with an unresponsive person. Talk to a partner about something important to you. As you speak, your partner is silent, averts his eyes, slowly moves away. Notice what your impulse is toward the person who doesn't listen. Do you feel like pushing him? Buttonholing him? Rejecting him?

Change roles and be aware of how you feel when you don't permit yourself to respond to someone. Do you resent him? Want to run away? Get closer to him? Do you have feelings of power over the other person, who must keep talking to fill the gap you've created?

Now play the game through a second time. This time touch the other person as he is speaking, and respond to what he is saying. *Vive la différence!*

Mutual Interview. Learn as much as you can about your partner in ten minutes. Ask him questions to find out the really important things about him. Then switch and have your partner interview you.

A variation of this is to interview each other in a single fifteen-minute period. Be aware of what is happening between you as the dual interview takes place: Who takes the initiative and how? Who talks more? Are you angry, resigned? What if the interview doesn't go the way you think it should?

Next, introduce your partner to the group, relating what you've learned about him. After all introductions have been made, have the group discuss whether the introductions contained really important information about each person. Note what you deem important to know about a person and how much about someone else you remember. Tell how the group could get to know and understand you better.

Touching Experience

Touching is a normal expression of interest and affection and can help you know someone in ways that words can't convey.

The importance of touch is conveyed in this moving account by Althea Horner, a psychotherapist:

"I was born to a mother who could be tender and demonstrative towards the helpless baby, but who withdrew love when the child's developing will led to the first 'no. . . .' I do not remember the last time I was held affectionately in my mother's arms. I grew up convinced that she did not love me, and questioned my lovability. Then I married a kind but undemonstrative man, who grew up in a home where open affection was not shown. My need for touch, for stroking, for contact comfort, was once again thwarted. My self-image became more and more one of being an 'untouchable.'

"As a graduate student, I went into psychotherapy, where, from time to time, I would express my longings to have the therapist hold me. Each time I was told that my problem was that I wanted gratification instead of therapy. Now I had learned something new about myself. Not only was I untouchable, but my wish for contact comfort was 'bad.' "

Then Mrs. Horner attended a workshop at Esalen led by Dr. Herbert A. Otto. Part of Dr. Otto's technique is the issuing of lapel buttons that indicate the individual's willingness to be touched. "Suddenly I found myself in a situation in which touch was neither bad nor feared, but valued and encouraged."

Later that week Mrs. Horner attended a workshop conducted by Virginia Satir, a specialist in family therapy. "Once more . . . I found myself being held like a child by its mother when, sensing my anguish, Mrs. Satir sat down on the floor beside me and gently held me in her arms. Men, women—it made no difference. The need for the kind of contact that says you are not untouchable, bad or dangerous has no sex."

Here are some games for getting acquainted through touch.

Rump Bump. With your eyes closed, slowly back in toward the center of the room. As you make contact with other backs, gently bump hello, and move on. After about a minute, stop next to one back, and get to know this back with your own. Have a back conversation: Try an argument; then be playful, tender. Do a back dance, exploring all kinds of motion. After five minutes, stop and be aware of each other; then gradually move apart. Experience how your back feels. Open your eyes, and look at your partner.

Slap Rap. Have a conversation by slapping your partner's arms and shoulders. Start the conversation by slapping with both hands simultaneously. Your partner answers. This goes back and forth like ordinary conversation.

Blind Milling. Walk about the room, with your eyes closed. When you find someone, explore him with your hands—touch his shoulders, face, hands, hair. Communicate with him just by touch. See if you can convey

a message about how you feel about him; let him communicate back. Now find a way to say good-bye. Continue milling until you bump into someone else, and touch-talk with him, too.

To get some perspective on the freedom offered by blind milling, try milling with your eyes open. Are you self-conscious? Distracted? Closed in? What accounts for the difference?

Hand Conversation. Here's a clear way of experiencing the two opposite extremes of conversations: normal cocktail-type chatter and the deeper talk of touch.

First, sit back to back with a partner, and talk about yourself. Very likely you'll find it hard to make gut contact. Most such talks, in which not even the eyes are in contact, stay on a superficial level: "How come you're here?" "What do you do for a living?"

After five minutes or so, take an opposite tack. Face each other, with your knees touching. Keeping your eyes closed, see how much you can express merely through touching each other's hands. Through touch alone you're likely to find an exchange consisting of warmth, interest, possibly anger and frustration, but nonetheless a great deal of feeling. One participant observed: "I never dreamt a conversation without words could be so intimate. Exploring a person's fingers can be like feeling between his legs."

Because of such lightning intimacy, and because of general proscriptions equating touch with sexuality, men sometimes find it difficult to have hand conversations with another man. If men are afraid of the homosexual overtones, it often helps to get started with aggressive rather than delicate emotions, and then gradually build up to more tender expressions. A variation on a hand conversation calls for a third person to suggest the emotions to be expressed: "Now express anger. . . . Now, pleading. . . . Now, irritation. . . . Now, concern." The idea is to point up the enormous range of feelings that can be expressed nonverbally.

I and Thou: Here is a touch exercise that may give you another dimension of experience with another person: a sense of oneness, of merging with the other.

Find a partner, with your eyes closed. With your left hand touch your own face; with your right hand touch your partner's face. Try to touch the same features of your face and your partner's at the same time. Do this for about five minutes. You're likely to get the sensation that two faces—indeed, two beings—have become one. Conversely, you may become more sensitive to the other as you become aware of the contrasts between you.

As a variation on this game, again close your eyes, and explore a partner's face with your fingers, as a blind man would. See if you can tell not only what he might look like, but also something of what he might be feeling. When you've explored each other's face, slowly open your eyes at the same time, and gaze into each other's eyes.

GETTING CLOSER

Dr. Sidney M. Jourard of the University of Florida has described two kinds of encounters: the encounter that mystifies, and the encounter that reveals.

The encounter that mystifies is illustrated by the young man on the make. His real intent is: "I want her to tumble for me," but he does not express it. Instead, he tries to mislead the girl as to his real intentions. Observes Dr. Jourard: "He will show aspects of himself that aim at persuading or influencing the other. The other person has been reduced from the status of a person to the status of an object, a manipulandum, something to be used if it is useful and neutralized or changed if it is not."

An encounter that mystifies invariably results in the maintaining of emotional distance. No genuine feeling is exchanged.

By contrast, the encounter that reveals brings you and another closer. "In genuine dialogue, each experiences the other as a person," noted Jourard. "Transparency, not mystification, is one of the goals. . . .The aim is to show oneself in willful honesty. . . .Dialogue is like mutual unveiling."

Whenever open and direct feeling is expressed and responded to in a relationship, a heightened feeling of closeness results. Realness is the soil out of which flower warmth and trust.

The following games will help you learn to be more open and direct in expressing your feelings.

First Impressions

Stand in front of another group member, and look him in the eye. Touch him if you'd like, and tell him as honestly and openly as you can what your first impression of him is.

Give your first impression of each group member in this fashion. Repeat until all group members have given their first impressions of each other. Ann was somewhat surprised when the impression of her was of a nice New England type, a good sister, bright, well organized. She thought of herself as a New York girl, artistic and somewhat nonconforming. But this image didn't come through.

After thinking about it, she realized she gave a stiff impression, that it was a part of herself that she often wanted to forget about. Yet her dress was a crisp classic shirtwaist, her eyes had a wide-open, innocent bright look, her talk was schoolmarmish. Who was she? This

game of First Impressions brought the question up with new immediacy.

How do the first impressions you have of a person compare with those that others in the group have of him? What do your impressions of others reveal about *you*? Simon's first impression of Myra was: "I see you as a dominating female, a real PTA-type, middle-aged authority figure."

Actually, Myra was a shy woman, only five years older than Simon and still in her thirties. Simon realized later that he felt threatened by her seeming competence—and that "with women who remind me of my mother I act like a little boy."

Deliberately seek out a person whom you *don't* like. Tell him in detail what you find dislikable in him.

Then reflect: What is there in him that you don't like about yourself?

"You're fat. You're ugly. You're disgusting." Alan's voice was thick with loathing toward Don, a shambling, overweight figure with thick eyeglasses and an inadequate air.

"Come on," a member of the group said. "Don's no beauty. But he's not that bad. What's bugging *you*? How does he make you feel?"

Alan thought a while.

"Embarrassed," he said at last.

"Embarrassed?"

"He reminds me of Milo Berryman."

"Who the hell is Milo Berryman?"

"The class creep when I was in elementary school," Alan explained. "I used to dread being associated with him, because I was embarrassed that people would think I was his friend. Don, it's not your problem. It's mine."

Silent Language

Accepting feeling. Fred's wife had just recently left him. He came to the group to get some feeling of closeness and to hear about the hurts of other people. Dr. Clark Moustakas in *Individuality and Encounter* noted that as Fred talked on and analyzed various people, he revealed himself to be defensive and sarcastic. Several participants told him that he was not able to take anything from the group.

"Go into the center, Fred," Moustakas told him. "Stop shielding yourself with words, and simply make yourself open to what each member of the group might feel like coming up to give you."

One person came up and massaged his shoulders. Someone else shook his hand. Someone else kissed him. One fellow had him lie down on his back and simply lay on top of him for a couple of minutes.

When they were through, Fred began to talk in a different tone as he recalled his loneliness as a child, and tears began to roll down his cheeks. For the first time this experience allowed him to open up his painful feelings to the group. He brought forth affectionate and caring responses from people who previously had been hostile to him.

Eyeballing. Sit facing a partner, and stare directly into each other's eyes for five minutes. Tell him something important with your eyes. See what he has to say to you.

Afterward, spend a few minutes talking about your experience. Typically, the talk will be more open and animated after the nonverbal encounter. The eyeball-to-eyeball meeting frees emotions by forcing you to *look* and make genuine contact with your partner. You'll find new truth in the old adage. The eyes are the windows of the soul.

Psychologist Paul Bindrim often asks participants in his workshops to spend five minutes talking with a partner, learning as much as possible about him, then five minutes gazing wordlessly into his eyes. Most participants report feeling they've learned much more about the other from the nonspeaking eye contact.

Hugging. An important part of group experiences is hugging. It can help a group feel closer and can physically express the warmth and affection the members feel toward one another. At the same time, hugging can develop into a ritual in which it becomes almost mandatory for every person to hug every other person. To keep the hug from becoming a cop-out, make sure you really feel like hugging. When you feel the urge to hug someone, express it. Sometimes a whole group wants to express its closeness by hugging. All members get as close as possible and put their arms around each other. Spontaneous swaying often develops.

One participant described his feelings about a group hug: "Six of us standing close in a circle with arms around each other, talking, caring. I have never known this much acceptance. It overwhelms me. They see—draw closer."

Pantomimes provide another nonverbal way of communicating with your partner. Pantomime your impressions of him. Do you like him? Are you put off by him? Show your feelings, with gestures and facial expressions.

Then pantomime how you feel your partner feels toward you. Afterward ask yourself: "Is this how I really feel toward myself?" These pantomimes often permit people to express feelings toward themselves and others that they would not ordinarily verbalize.

Alice, a retired schoolteacher, liked her partner, a housewife named Joanie, and sought to tell Joanie, "I'm very fond of you," in pantomime. In the discussion afterward Joanie said, "I disgust you, don't I?" As the woman talked, Alice realized that she had a lot of difficulty expressing warmth persuasively. Moreover, it occurred to her that she was often oblivious of other

people's feelings: she had not noticed the look of hurt on Joanie's face.

Joanie, on the other hand, also found a lot to think about, since she had interpreted Alice's positive expression as being one of disgust. She concluded that she was frequently suspicious of other people's claiming they liked her, since she had a fairly low opinion of herself.

Joanie and Alice continued on to the next step, in which you express how you think your partner sees you. Joanie puffed up her cheeks and expanded her arms in front of her belly pantomiming fatness. In reality, she was reasonably trim. But she had been a fat child and teen-ager—and now, though in her early forties, she carried around a corpulent afterimage of herself that she loathed.

Straight Talk

The object of these games is to help you verbalize your feelings, expectations, fears, hopes, problems—to help you talk to people about things that really matter to you.

What Do You Want? Keep asking your partner one and only one question: "What do you want?" Say this with many different inflections and gestures as your partner keeps trying to answer the question. Then switch roles. Answer with respect to what you want at *this* moment.

This experiment can help you sharpen your perception of the ever-changing flow of wants and desires that exist in you. It can also help you express these wants to another person.

One man's list of responses to "What do you want?" was as follows:

"I want to take a deep breath."
"I want you to leave me alone."
"I want to love my wife more."
"I want to go to bed with Muriel [a girl in the group]."
"I want to laugh."
"I want to cry."
"I want you to turn around."
"I want to walk in the country."

When I Grow Up. Share your fantasies of what you would like to do and be. Such fantasies are not always as impractical as they seem. One young accountant said that his boyhood wish had always been to become a deep-sea diver. He expected derision, since his parents had always laughed. But instead he got encouragement. "You have only one life," said a group member, "so you really ought to do what you want." The young man thereafter began training for a career as a diver.

Major Event. All members of a group share with one another the most significant moments of their lives, happy and sad.

In one group an elderly man talked about having his

face destroyed in an automobile accident and then surgically reconstructed.

This was the first time he'd ever exposed how he felt about living a life disfigured by scar tissue. When he finished, several members who previously could not bear to look at him now found they could gaze at him with genuine warmth.

Current Problem. One member relates a problem that represents a pervasive threat in his life. Other members listen carefully, asking questions and offering suggestions.

Sharing Games. Share with the group:

> an incident from your childhood that was deeply formative.
>
> your happiest moment.
>
> your most embarrassing moment.
>
> a personal secret.
>
> your feelings about the part of your body that you like the most, that you like the least.
>
> how you feel about your work—its satisfactions and frustrations.
>
> how you feel about your financial situation, income, savings, debts.
>
> your love life, past and present.
>
> your problems in marriage, its daily annoyances.
> you and your partner's basic differences.
>
> your feelings about other members of the group. . . .

GAMES FOR MERRIMENT

These games are just for fun. They can be hilarious. Try one of these games as a relief from a series of exercises involving grief, anger or fear. They have also proved useful in drawing together a group whose members have been ill at ease.

Chucklebelly

Everybody lies in a circle on the floor. Each person lies with his head on the belly of someone else. The first person goes, "Ha." The second, "Ha-ha." The third "Ha-ha-ha." And so on, around the group. Usually shrieks of resounding laughter ensue, and the effect heightens as people laugh at the laughter.

Human Carpet

Everybody lies on the floor side by side, with their shoes off. For snugness, they lie head to foot. The person on the end rolls on top of this human carpet. When he gets to the end, he lies down, and the next person goes, until everyone has a roll.

People Machine

In this game members of a group make themselves into a machine—with as many moving gears and levers as they can devise. One member starts by repeatedly doing a movement, like shaking a leg and making a sound. Another member joins himself to him and starts his own motion. A third attaches himself, and so on. Ultimately the group looks and sounds like a Rube Goldberg machine.

Tangle

Everyone stands side by side and clasps the hand of the person next to him. The person on one end of the row becomes the leader. He starts weaving through the other people—between them, under their legs, around them—until he can take the hand of the person on the other end.

Still holding hands, everyone follows him. There will soon be a horrendous tangle. The object of the game is to unravel the snarl and end up in a circle without unclasping hands. It may be necessary to appoint a traffic cop to call out who should lift up which leg or come around whose head.

Pile-Up

Members of the group lie on their bellies in a large circle, heads pointing toward the center. With their eyes closed, they begin crawling toward the center. They will bump into one another or crawl over others. Everyone continues to crawl until he reaches the center, where a pile will start to form. When everyone is part of the pile, all open their eyes and look around.

Symphony Orchestra

Make a piece of music as a group—but without using any instruments except your voices and bodies. One person may begin by slapping someone else's belly and buttocks, while chirping. Another might join in by clapping a partner's hands and chanting. A third might click his teeth together, and so on. Change the rhythm and your action as the mood changes.

Fred Hamil
do-it-yourself propaganda

The Officer Bob Drawing Book is widely distributed in grade schools by the police officials of a Southwestern state; variations on this theme appear in many public school systems throughout the U.S.

Artist Fred Hamil took the propogandists at their word and reacted, drawing what *he* saw. We call it adult show and tell.

Media is limited only by the range of our imaginations. Perhaps you might explore some of the possibilities found in this Drawing Book.

OFFICER BOB
Drawing BOOK

Draw yourself in the picture
with our friend Officer Bob

MY NAME _____

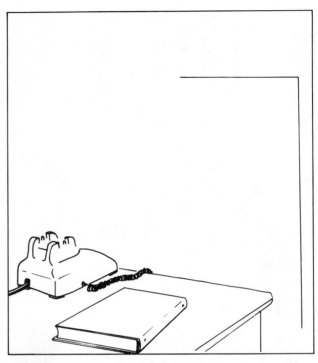

You can be the eyes and ears of the Police Department. If you observe suspicious persons or happenings, ask your parents to report this to the Police by calling 885-1222. Draw yourself reporting a suspicious person to the Police.

Policemen work in every part of town each day, helping people. Draw Officer Bob driving down the street in his police car. Draw yourself watching him.

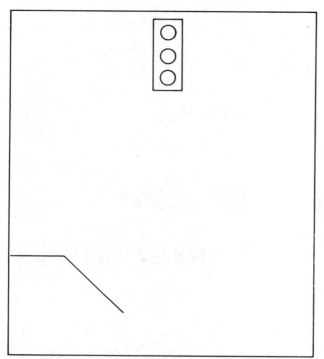

Some Policemen help direct traffic. Draw Officer Bob helping you cross a busy street.

Some Policemen help direct traffic. Draw Officer Bob helping you cross a busy street.

right you are if you say you are – obscurely

from TIME Magazine

Most of us worry about making our ideas clear. Here is an alternative point of view.

The scene is the office of the dean of admissions at Instant College. A pale adolescent approaches the dean, who is appropriately clad in flowing white memos.

Student: Y-you sent for me, sir?

Dean: Yes, my boy. We've decided to accept you as a student here at Instant.

Student: Sir, I can't tell you how pleased I am. I mean, my high school average is 65, I got straight Ds in mathematics, confuse the Norman Conquest with D-day, have a sub-average IQ, and got turned down by every other college in America. yet in spite of all of this, you've accepted me.

Dean: Not in spite of it, boy! Because of it!

Student: (*dimly*): Sir?

Dean: Don't you see? You're a challenge. We're starting with nothing—you. Yet before we're through, corporations will seek your advice, little magazines will print your monographs on such arcane subjects as forensic medicine and epistemology, newspapers will publish your utterances as you enplane for conferences abroad.

Student: Me?

Dean: You. Because you will be an Expert.

Student: An expert what?

Dean: Just an Expert.

Student: But sir, I don't know anything and I can't learn much. Not in four years, anyway.

Dean: Why, my boy, we'll have you out of here in an hour. All you need is the catalyst that instantly transforms the lowest common denominator, you, into an Expert.

Student: Money? Power? Intellect? Charm?

Dean: No. These things are but children's toys compared to Jargon.

Student: Jargon?

Dean: (*turning to his textbook*): The dictionary calls it "confused, unintelligible language: gibberish, a dialect regarded as barbarous or outlandish." But we at Instant call it the Expert's Ultimate Weapon. In 1967, it will hypnotize friends, quash enemies and intimidate whole nations. Follow me.

A school bell rings, and the entire faculty enters: Dr. Gummidge, professor of sociology; the Rev. Mr. Logos, head of the theological seminary; Dr. Beazle, head of the medical school;...Dr. Gummidge steps forward, conducts the student to an uncomfortable chair, mills about him like a lonely crowd, and begins.

Gummidge: Remember Gummidge's Law and you will never be Found Out: The amount of expertise varies in inverse proportion to the number of statements understood by the General Public.

Student: In other words?

Gummidge: In other words, never say "in other words." That will force you to clarify your statements. Keep all pronunciamentos orotund and hazy. Suppose your mother comes to school and asks how you are doing. Do I reply: "He is at the bottom of his class—lazy and good-for-nothing"?

Student: Why not? Everyone else does.

Gummidge: I am not everyone else. I reply: "The student in question is performing minimally for his peer group and is an emerging under-achiever."

Student: Wow!

Gummidge: Exactly. If you are poor, I refer to you as disadvantaged; if you live in a slum, you are in a culturally deprived environment.

Student: If I want to get out of a crowded class?

Gummidge: You seek a more favorable pupil-teacher ratio, plus a decentralized learning center in the multiversity.

Student: If I'm learning a language by conversing in it?

Gummidge: That's the aural-oral method. Say it aloud.

The student does and is completely incomprehensible. A cheer goes up from the faculty.

Gummidge: From now on; you must never speak; you must verbalize.

Student: Must I verbalize Jargon only to my peer group?

Gummidge: Not at all. You can now use it even when addressing pre-schoolers. In his book *Translations from the English,* Robert Paul Smith offers these samples: "He shows a real ability in plastic conception." That means he can make a snake out of clay. "He's rather slow in group integration and reacts negatively to aggressive stimulus." He cries easily. And "He does seem to have developed late in large-muscle control." He falls on his head frequently.

Student: (*awestruck*): I'll never be able to do it.

Gummidge: Of course you will. The uninitiated are easily impressed. It's all rather like the ignorant woman who learns that her friend's son has graduated from medical school. "How's your boy?" she asks. The friend clucks sadly: "He's a practicing homosexual." "Wonderful!" cries the first. "Where's his office?" Do I make myself clear?

Student: No, sir.

Gummidge: Fine. Now open your textbook to the David Riesman chapter. Here is the eminent sociologist writing about Jargon: "Phrases such as 'achievement-oriented' or 'need-achievement' were, if I am not mistaken, invented by colleagues and friends of mine, Harry Murray and David C. McClelland...It has occurred to me that they may be driven by a kind of asceticism precisely because they are poetic men of feeling who...have chosen to deal with soft data in a hard way."...See how complicated you can make things? Imagine what damage you can wreak in the schools where a situation is no longer practical, it is viable; where a pupil is no longer unmanageable, but alienated. Get it?

Student: Got it.

Gummidge: Do books have words and pictures?

Student: No, sir, they have verbal symbols and visual representations.

Gummidge: You're on your way. For your final exam, read and commit to memory the 23rd Psalm Jargonized by Alan Simpson, president of Vassar College.

Student (*droning*): "The Lord is my external-internal integrative mechanism. I shall not be deprived of gratifications for my viscerogenic hungers or my need-dispositions. He motivates me to orient myself towards a nonsocial object with effective significance."

The student falls into a dreamlike trance during which Professor Gummidge tiptoes off and is replaced by the Rev. Mr. Logos, who continues the psalm.

Logos: "He positions me in a nondecisional situation. He maximizes my adjustment..." (*As the student wakes up*): I'm the Reverend Mr. Logos. Bless you, my son.

Student: I see you're wearing a turned-around collar and a *yarmulke.* Just what is your religion?

Logos: I am a theologian. Does that answer you?

Student: No.

Logos: Splendid. How would you refer to a priest disagreeing with a minister?

Student: As two guys arguing?

Logos: No, no, no! Religious leaders never argue, they have dialogues, or I-Thou relationships.

Student: If their studies are mainly about Jesus?

Logos: They are Christocentrically oriented. If they are interpreting the Bible, hermeneutics is the term.

Student: Can you predict what words will be In for the theological year ahead?

Logos: Certainly. Demythologizing, optimism, theology of hope, *engagé* and commitment.

Student: I like dialectic theology and conceptualism.

Logos: Forget them. They're all Out. Concentrate on phenomenology, sociological inspiration, ethical activism, crisis of authority.

Student: Suppose someone realizes that I don't have the faintest idea what I'm talking about?

Logos: Then accuse him of objectification. If he doesn't go away, ask him what he did before he got religion, before his ultimate faith-concern, or better still. *Selbstverständnis.*

Student: But that's not even English.

Logos: All the better. Many influential theologians wrote in German— Bultmann, Bonhoeffer, Barth— and German not only offers us a chance to obfuscate, it adds a tangy foreign flavor...

Student (*writing furiously*): Are you sure Jargon *really* works? In religion, I mean?

Logos: Does it? I quote from a distinguished cleric: "I can't make heads or tails out of a great deal of what Tillich says." The confessor is Dr. Billy Graham himself.

At this, the Rev. Mr. Logos is borne away by the laity to edit a book of his sermons entitled Through Exegesis and Hermeneutics We Arrive at Kerygma. *In his place steps Dr. Beazle, who takes the student's blood pressure, temperature, hemoglobin count and wallet.*

Beazle: Now what kind of medical career do you want, physical or psychiatric?

Student: I don't know. I never thought about it.

Beazle: That's a good start. Suppose we begin with plain everyday medicine. Was it not Herman Melville who wrote: "A man of true science uses but few hard words, and those only when none other will answer his purpose; whereas the smatterer in science thinks that by mouthing hard words he proves that he understands hard things." Now you don't want to be an ordinary man of true science when you can be a full-fledged Smatterer, do you?

Student: I guess not.

Beazle: Very well, remember never to let the patient be fully aware of what is wrong. Even tonsillitis can be described as a malign hypertrophied condition that affects nares and pharynx and may result in paraphonia clausa. It was I, you know, who wrote the sign seen in hospitals: "Illumination is required to be extinguished on these premises on the termination of daily activities."

Student: Which means—

Beazle: Put out the lights when you leave.

Student: Marvelous.

Beazle: It was nothing, really. We medical men have been confounding patients for years. As far back as 1699, the physician and poet Samuel Garth wrote: "The patient's ear remorseless, he assails/Murders with jargon where his medicine fails." Still, physical medicine is nothing compared with psychiatry. There's where we Jargonists truly have our day. Suppose a man loses his wife and is unable to love anyone because he is sad. What do I tell him?

Student: Cheer up, there are lots of fish in the—?

Beazle (interrupting): Of course not. I intone: You have suffered an object loss in which you had an over-cathesis of libido and have been unable to decathect the libido and invest it in a new object. Do you follow me?

Student: I think so.

Beazle: Then be warned: the public is on our trail; they now have learned the meanings of the "oses" and the "itises." You had better replace them with "inadequacies," and "dependencies," tell the man who acts out fantasies that he is "role playing," speak of the creation of a child as "exclusive electivity of dynamic specificity."

Student: And when the child is born?

Beazle: His development proceeds through "mutual synthesis carried on through a functional zone of mutuality."

Student: In short, he grows up.

Beazle: In long, he proceeds in a continuous unidirectional ever-varying interplay of organism and environment.

Student: If a patient is unhappy?

Beazle: He is having an identity crisis.

Student: But suppose he's just unhappy?

Beazle: No one is just unhappy. Psych harder!

Student: I'll start immediately. I will follow Lionel Trilling's dictum: no one will fall in love and get married as long as I'm present.

Beazle: What will they do?

Student: Their libidinal impulses being reciprocal, they will integrate their individual erotic drives and bring them within the same frame of reference. How am I doing?

Beazle: Not badly, but I can still understand you.

Student: Sorry. Day by day I will grow more obscure, until my patients and I completely fail to communicate.

Beazle: Oh, if only I could believe that! Smog, confuse, obfuscate!...

Dean (handing the student a diploma printed on sheeplike vinyl): We've done all we can for you, son. In George Orwell's paraphrase: "The race is not to the swift—nor the battle to the strong...but time and chance—"

Student: I know. "Objective considerations of contemporary phenomena compels the conclusion that success or failure in competitive activities exhibits no tendency to be commensurate with innate capacity, but that a considerable element of the unpredictable must be taken into account."

Dean: Exactly. (*Moist of eye, he pats the new graduate on the head.*) You can now take your pick of careers in medicine, religion, business and geopolitics—as well as wine-tasting and art criticism. And if you fail at everything, there's a job for you at Instant College. (*Calling after him as the student exits.*) And remember, it is better to curse one candle than to light the darkness...

He extinguishes the lights, leaving the audience in blackness as

THE CURTAIN FALLS

communicode 2

Judy L. Haynes

For information on how to solve a Communicode, see page 63. Communicode 2 uses a new code. If you have difficulty getting started, a solving clue is on page 124. The answer is on page 132.

FROM THE PODIUM
Example: Commencement Address

CIFUQ — LNTTUQ
  KAUUHP

ICQUMURR
  KAUUHP

AUQKSCKNBU
  KAUUHP

KUQEJT

RUHFSQU

JQCFNJT

CTTJSTHUEUTF

NTCSDSQCR
  CLLQUKK

KCRUK
  ANFHP

USRJDG

If you're still in the puzzle-solving frame of mind, there's one last puzzle on page 127.

IS LANGUAGE SEXIST?

Casey Miller and Kate Swift

The English language puts women down! So why must we take it like a man?

A *riddle* is making the rounds that goes like this: A man and his young son were in an automobile accident. The father was killed and the son, who was critically injured, was rushed to a hospital. As attendants wheeled the unconscious boy into the emergency room, the doctor on duty looked down at him and said, "My God, it's my son!" What was the relationship of the doctor to the injured boy?

If the answer doesn't jump to your mind, another riddle that has been around a lot longer might help: The blind beggar had a brother. The blind beggar's brother died. The brother who died had no brother. What relation was the blind beggar to the blind beggar's brother?

As with all riddles, the answers are obvious once you see them: The doctor was the boy's mother and the beggar was her brother's sister. Then why doesn't everyone solve them immediately? Mainly because our language, like the culture it reflects, is male-oriented. To say that a woman in medicine is an exception is simply to confirm that statement. Thousands of doctors are women, but in order to be seen in the mind's eye, they must be called women doctors.

Except for words that refer to females by definition (mother, actress, congresswoman), and words for occupations traditionally held by females (nurse, secretary, prostitute), the English language defines everyone as male. The hypothetical person ("If a man can walk ten miles in two hours..."), the average person ("the man in the street"), and the active person ("the man on the move") are male. The assumption is that unless otherwise identified, people in general—including doctors and beggars—are men. As the beetle-browed and mustachioed man in a Steig cartoon says to his two male drinking companions, "When I speak of mankind, one thing I don't mean is womankind."

Semantically speaking, woman is not one with the species of man, but a distinct subspecies. "Man," says the 1971 edition of the *Britannica Junior Encyclopaedia,* "is the highest form of life on earth. His superior intelligence, combined with certain physical characteristics, have enabled man to achieve things that are impossible for other animals." As though quoting the Steig character, still speaking to his friends in McSorley's, the *Junior Encyclopaedia* continues: "Man must invent most of his behavior, because he lacks the instincts of lower animals. . . .Most of the things he learns have been handed down from his ancestors by language and symbols rather than by biological inheritance."

Considering that for the last five thousand years society has been patriarchal, that statement explains a lot. It explains why Eve was made from Adam's rib instead of the other way around and who invented all those Adam-rib words like female and woman in the first place. This inheritance through language and other symbols begins in the home (also called a man's castle) where man and wife (not husband and wife, or man and woman) live for a while with their children. It is reinforced by religious training, the educational system, the press, Government, commerce, and the law.

Consider some of the examples of language and symbols in American history. When schoolchildren learn from their textbooks that the early colonists gained valuable experience in governing themselves, they are not told that the early colonists who were women were denied the privilege of self-government; when they learn that in the eighteenth century the average man had to manufacture many of the things he and his family needed, they are not told that this "average man" was often a woman who manufactured much of what she and her family needed. Young people learn that intrepid pioneers crossed the country in covered wagons with their wives, children, and cattle; they do not learn that women themselves were intrepid pioneers rather than part of the baggage.

Sexist language is any language that expresses such stereotyped attitudes and expectations or assumes the inherent superiority of one sex over the other. When a woman says of her husband, who has drawn up plans for a new bedroom wing and left out closets, "Just like a man," her language is as sexist as the man's who says, after his wife has changed her mind about needing the new wing after all, "Just like a woman."

Male and female are not sexist words, but masculine and feminine are as sexist as any words can be, since it is almost impossible to use them without invoking cultural stereotypes. When people construct lists of "masculine" and "feminine" traits they almost always end up making assumptions that have nothing to do with innate differences between the sexes. We have a friend who happens to be going through the process of pinning down this very phenomenon. He is seven years old and his question concerns why his coats and shirts button left over right while his sister's button the other way. He assumes it must have something to do with the differences between boys and girls, but he can't see how.

What our friend has yet to grasp is that the way you button your coat, like most sex-differentiated customs, has nothing to do with real differences but much to do with what society wants you to feel about yourself as a male or female person. Society decrees that it is appropriate for girls to dress differently from boys, to act differently, and to think differently. Boys must be masculine, whatever that means, and girls must be feminine.

Unabridged dictionaries are a good source for finding out what society decrees to be appropriate, though less by definition than by their choice of association and illustrations. Words associated with males—"manly," "virile," and "masculine," for example—are defined through a broad range of positive attributes like strength, courage, directness, and independence, and they are illustrated through such examples of contemporary usage as "a manly determination to face what comes," "a virile literary style," " a masculine love of sports." Corresponding words associated with females are defined with fewer attributes (though weakness is often one of them), and the examples given are generally negative if not clearly pejorative: "feminine wiles," "womanish tears," "a woman-like lack of promptness," "convinced that drawing was a waste of time, if not downright womanly."

One dictionary, after defining the word "womanish" as "suitable to or resembling a woman," further defines it as "unsuitable to a man or to a strong character of either sex." Words derived from "sister" and "brother" provide another apt example, for whereas "sissy," applied either to a male or female, conveys the message that sisters are expected to be timid and cowardly, "buddy" makes clear that brothers are friends.

The subtle disparagement of females and corresponding approbation of males wrapped up in many English words is painfully illustrated by "tomboy." Here is an instance where a girl who likes sports and the out-of-doors, who is curious about how things work, who is adventurous and bold instead of passive, is defined in terms of something she is not—a boy. By denying that she can be the person she is and still be a girl, the word surreptitiously undermines her sense of identity: it says she is unnatural. A "tomboy," as defined by one dictionary, is a "girl, especially a young girl who behaves like a spirited boy." But who makes the judgment that she is acting like a spirited boy, not a spirited girl? Can it be a coincidence that in the case of the dictionary just quoted the editor, executive editor, managing editor, general manager, all six members of the Board of Linguists, the usage editor, science editor, all six general editors of definitions, and ninety-four out of the 104 distinguished experts consulted on usage—are men?

Possibly because of the negative images associated with womanish or woman-like, and with expressions like "woman driver," and "woman of the street," the word woman dropped out of fashion for a time. The women of the office and the women on the assembly line and the women one knew in school all became ladies, girls or gals. Now a countermovement supported by the very term Women Liberation is putting back into words like woman and sister and sisterhood, the meaning they were losing by default. It is as though, in the nick of time, women had seen that the language itself could destroy them. . . .

What women have been called in the press—or at least the part that operates above ground—is only a fraction of the infinite variety of alternatives to "woman" used in the subcultures of the English-speaking world. Beyond "chicks," "dolls," "dames," "babes," "skirts," and "broads" are the words and phrases in which women are reduced to their sexuality and nothing more. It would be hard to think of another area of language in which the human mind has been so fertile in devising and borrowing abusive terms. In *The Female Eunuch,* Germaine Greer devotes four pages to anatomical terms and words for animals, vegetables, fruits, baked goods, implements, and receptacles, all of which are used to dehumanize the female person. Jean Faust, in an article aptly called "Words That Oppress," suggests that the effort to diminish women through language is rooted in a male fear of sexual inadequacy. "Woman is made to feel guilty for and akin to natural disasters," she writes. "Hurricanes and typhoons are named after her. Any negative or threatening force is given a feminine name. If a man runs into bad luck climbing up the ladder of success (a male-invented game), he refers to the 'bitch goddess' success."

The sexual overtones in the ancient and no doubt honorable custom of calling ships "she" have become more explicit and less honorable in an age of air travel: "I'm Karen. Fly me." Attitudes of ridicule, contempt, and disgust toward female sexuality have spawned a rich glossary of insults and epithets not found in dictionaries. And the usage in which four-letter words meaning copulate are interchangeable with cheat, attack, and destroy can scarcely be unrelated to the savagery of rape.

When words are suggested like "herstory" (for history), "hissicane" (for hurricane), and "mistresspiece" (for the work of a Virginia Woolf) one suspects a not-too-subtle attempt to make the whole language problem look silly. But unless Alexander Pope, when he wrote "The proper study of mankind is man," meant that women should be relegated to the footnotes (or, as George Orwell might have put it, "All men are equal, but men are more equal than women"), viable new words will surely someday supersede the old.

Without apologies to Freud, the great majority of women do not wish in their hearts that they were men. If having grown up with a language that tells them they are at the same time men and not men raises psychic doubts for women, the doubts are not of their sexual identity but of their human identity. Perhaps the present unrest surfacing in the women's movement is part of an evolutionary change in our particular form of life—the one form of all in the animal and plant kingdoms that orders and interprets its reality by symbols. The achievements of the species called man have brought us to the brink of self-destruction. If the species survives into the next century with the expectation of going on, it may only be because we have become part of what science writer Harlow Shapley calls the psychozoic kingdom, where brain overshadows brawn and rationality has replaced superstition.

Searching the roots of Western civilization for a word to call this new species of man and woman, someone might come up with "gen," as in genesis and generic. With such a word, "man" could be used exclusively for males as "woman" is used for females, for gen would include both sexes. Like the words deer and bison, gen would be both plural and singular. Gen would express the warmth and generalized sexuality of generous, gentle, and genuine: the specific sexuality of genital and genetic. In the new family of gen, girls and boys would grow to genhood, and to speak of genkind would be to include all the people of the earth.

THE TYRANNY OF WOMEN'S LIBERATION

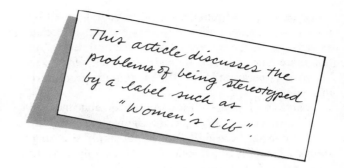

This article discusses the problems of being stereotyped by a label such as "Women's Lib".

Corinne Geeting

It's not that I am against the liberation of women. God forbid! For years I have been working with groups dedicated to the goals of upgrading women's status, man dating prestige and policy-making positions for them in politics and higher education, establishing child-care centers to help solve their personal dilemmas as homemakers—in other words, working to make them first-class citizens. But only recently have I been criticized for my activities.

Now when I meet old friends, especially men, they say, "Well, how's Women's Liberation coming along?" And suddenly there is that edge in the voice, that look in the eye, and all the other metalanguage signals that suggest that I am "one of them." Suddenly I am a militant, a disrupter of the system, an enemy of the womanly. I am a victim of "Women's Liberation."

I imagine thousands of women in America are suffering the pangs of this outrageous fortune along with me, and I just want to spell out the problem as I see it because I believe it has been overlooked by most people, including many women who have been victimized. Strangely enough, those who consider themselves members of Women's liberation, or "Lib," are more often than not, I have found, not militant, wild-eyed, nor violent. They are victims of a public image of what a Woman Liberationist is.

Recently I agreed to appear on a local television show during which, as a representative of such groups as the American Association of University Women, the Business and Professional Women, and YWCA, I talked with a member of the local campus Women's Lib group. In introducing us, the emcee mentioned that the community wanted a discussion of the Women's Liberation Movement and that he had brought together two women who might be called members of that movement—one militant, the other less so. That was all it took for several hundred viewers to fix me with the image of Bra Burner, Man Hater, and Home Wrecker. None of these labels would have been appropriate to either of us females who were waiting to have a friendly exchange of mutual concerns. Since that occasion I have suffered from having associated myself with the Women's Liberation term. Even one eleven-year-old with better judgment than most viewers told me that he personally thought I was rather nice lady but, even so, I had a "liberal chin."

Although I have more areas of agreement than disagreement with many women who call themselves members of Women's Liberation, I am taking care now to make my position clear. To be called a Women's Liberation member is to become a victim of "the killing abstraction." Abstractions assault the mind, condition perceptions, establish authority, reward and punish—and enslave—those under their jurisdiction...

"Liberation" is fast becoming synonymous with walk-outs, sit-ins, protests, marches, even violence—no matter whether or not those in movements using this terminology are participants in any of these often bizarre efforts to correct social ills. "Women's Liberation" is becoming a band-wagon slogan, and I do not choose to be on any band-wagon. I want to be emancipated, independent, delivered from manipulation, and I want the same emancipation for everyone, male and female. I want to be unfettered by attitudes, images, inferred life styles, and all other aspects of a stereotyped label that threaten to dominate and control individuals. The very term "women's liberation" is creating a counter-productive movement.

Therefore, I suggest that women of courage and self-assurance should separate themselves carefully from the term. "Carefully" does not imply shouting, militancy, or irrational behavior. "Carefully" means explaining that Women's Liberation is a label, a beautiful example of the unbelievable power of words to control and misdirect human beings in their unguarded moments.

Recently I found, in my modest research, that the term "women's liberation" is relatively new. Betty Friedan did not use it in her classic, *The Feminine Mystique;* nor did Caroline Bird in *Born Female,* published in 1968. Not until the early 1970's did the category appear in *The Reader's Guide to Periodical Literature,* when only three articles were listed under "Women's Liberation," all of these written in late 1969. Checking these three, I found that the "movement" had sprung up no more than two or three years earlier, when Women's Liberation sud-

denly claimed recognition as titular head of the entire historical thrust to attain first-class citizenship for women...

When people ask me if I am "for" Women's Liberation, I tell them I am not going to be caught in the trap of saying either yes or no; I am not going to be either for or against anything that is such a generalization. We must begin by defining terms.

I am, however, considerably alarmed that "women's liberation"—the term itself—may be captured by political activists, militants, enraged men and women who read into that term license to tear down institutions, to destroy the constructive work that has been done toward the emancipation of women. How long will it be before the Medusa head of Women's Liberation will speak for the goddess of wisdom? This may be the greatest threat to their long, noble effort to achieve equality that women have yet faced in this country. The fallacy is rampant that Women's Liberation is the sum total of a great movement toward developing woman's full potential. We need to recognize the sinister power of a two-word label to paralyze the magnificent mainstream of that movement for American women.

SOLVING CLUE FOR COMMUNICODE 2

C = A; T = N; F = T

Hearing is a Way of Touching

John Kord Lagemann

Most people with perfectly normal hearing don't listen very effectively. We can gain much more from the sense of hearing than we normally do. At times, hearing can even serve as a psychological substitute for touching. Read on.

Our world is filled with sounds we never hear. The human auditory range is limited to begin with: if we could hear sounds lower than 20 vibrations per second, we would be driven mad by the rumblings and creakings of our muscles, intestines and heartbeats; every step we take would sound like an explosion. But even within our auditory range we select, focus, pay attention to a few sounds and blot out the rest. We are so assaulted by sound that we continually "turn off." But in the process we shut out the glorious symphony of sound in which the living world is bathed.

Everything that moves makes a sound, so all sounds are witnesses to events. Thus sound is a kind of fourth dimension, telling us what is going on, revealing nuances and complexities opaque to vision alone. If touch is the most personal of senses, then hearing—an outgrowth of the sense of touch, a highly specialized way of touching at a distance—is the most *social* of the senses.

The sound-tormented city dweller who habitually "turns off his audio" loses a dimension of social reality. Some people, for example, possess the ability to enter a crowded room and from the sounds encountered know immediately the mood, pace and direction of the group assembled. Everything becomes more real when heard as well as seen. It is, in fact, quite hard really to know a person by sight alone, without hearing his voice. And it is not just the sound of the voice that informs. Even the rhythm of footsteps reveals age and variations of mood—elation, depression, anger, joy.

For these reasons, hearing has a kind of primacy for the social being called man. A baby responds to sound before he does to sight, smell or taste. There is good evidence that the human fetus listens to its mother's heartbeats weeks before birth. This may explain why babies are easily lulled to sleep by rhythm, and why their first words are repeated syllables—*da-da, ma-ma, gee-gee*—that sound like the *lub-dub* of the heartbeat.

All through life, hearing is a major channel of experience, a more vital stimulus than vision. It is also the watchdog sense. Since there is no sound without movement of some kind taking place, sounds warn us of happenings. When we go to sleep, our perception of sound seems to be the last door to close, and the first to reopen as we awaken. Even as we sleep, the brain is alerted by certain key sounds. A mother wakes at the whimper of her baby. The average person is quickly roused by the sound of his own name.

Watchdog, stimulator, arouser—it is not surprising that modern urban man has turned down and even crippled this most stressful of senses. But hearing can also soothe and comfort. The snapping of logs in the fireplace, the gossipy whisper of a broom, the inquisitive wheeze of a drawer opening—all are savored sounds that make us feel at home. In a well-loved home, every chair produces a different, recognizable creak, every window a different click, groan or squeak. The kitchen by itself is a source of many pleasing sounds—the clop-clop of batter stirred in a crockery bowl, the chortle of simmering soup, the conversational maundering of an electric percolator on the breakfast table. Every place, every event has a sound dimension.

The sense of hearing can perhaps be restored to modern man if he better understands its worth and how it works. Most people would be surprised to discover how far the sense can be pushed by cultivation. At a friend's house recently my wife opened her purse and some coins spilled out, one after another onto the bare floor. "Three quarters, two dimes, a nickel and three pennies," said our host as he came in from the next room. And, as an afterthought: "One of the quarters is silver." He was right, down to the last penny.

"How did you do it?" we asked.

"Try it yourself," he said. We did and with a little practice we found it easy.

On the way home, my wife and I took turns closing our eyes and listening to the sound of our taxi on the wet street as it reflected from cars parked along the curb. Just from the sound we were able to tell small foreign cars from larger American cars. Such games are one of the best ways to open up new realms of hearing experience.

An allied beneficence of hearing is that "extrasensory" faculty of the blind called facial vision. Doctors have long marveled at this sensitivity to reflected sound. About 200 years ago, Erasmus Darwin, grandfather of Charles Darwin, reported a visit by a blind friend, one Justice Fielding. "He walked into my room for the first time and, after speaking a few words, said, 'This room is about 22 feet long, 18 wide and 12 high'—all of which he guessed by the ear with great accuracy."

Sound engineers call it "ambience," the impression we all get in some degree from sound waves bouncing off walls, trees, even people. For a blind person to interpret the echoes effectively, he uses a tapping cane, preferably with a tip of metal, nylon or other substance that produces a distinct, consistent sound. (Wood gives a different sound wet than dry.) The metal noisemaker called a "cricket" is equally effective. Animals, both terrestrial and non-terrestrial, also use "echo-location." The bat, for example, emits a very high-pitched sound and picks up echoes from any obstacle, even as thin as a human hair.

The human ear is an amazing mechanism. Though its inner operating parts occupy less than a cubic inch, it can distinguish from 300,000 to 400,000 variations of tone and intensity. The loudest sound it can tolerate is a trillion times more intense than the faintest sounds it can pick up—the dropping of the proverbial pin, the soft thud of falling snowflakes. When the eardrums vibrate in response to sound, the tiny piston-like stirrup bones of the middle ear amplify the vibrations. This motion is passed along to the snail-like chamber of the inner ear, which is filled with liquid and contains some 30,000 fibers. These fibers are made to bend, depending on the frequency of the vibration—shorter strands respond to higher wave-lengths, longer strands to lower—and this movement is translated into nerve impulses and sent to the brain, which then, somehow, "hears."

While we are still under age 30, most of us can hear tones as high as 20,000 cycles per second (c.p.s.), about five times as high as the highest C on a piano. With age, the inner ear loses its elasticity. It is unusual for a person over 40 to hear well above 10,000 c.p.s. He can still function, of course, since most conversation is carried on within an octave or two of middle C, or about 260 c.p.s.

Curiously, evidence indicates that people need sound. When we are lost in thought, we involuntarily drum with our fingers or tap with a pencil—a reminder that we are still surrounded by a world outside ourselves. Just cutting down *reflected* sound can produce some odd results. The nearest thing on earth to the silence of outer space, for example, is the "anechoic chamber" at the Bell Telephone Laboratories in Murray Hills, N.J., which is lined with material that absorbs 99.98 percent of all reflected sound. Men who have remained in the room for more than an hour report that they feel jittery and out of touch with reality.

One remarkable quality of the human ear is its ability to pick out a specific sound or voice from a surrounding welter of sound, and to locate its position. Toscanini, rehearsing a symphony orchestra of almost 100 musicians, unerringly singled out the oboist who slurred a phrase. "I hear a mute somewhere on one of the second violins," he said another time in stopping a rehearsal. Sure enough, a second violinist far back on the stage discovered that he had failed to remove his mute.

We owe our ability to zero in on a particular sound to the fact that we have two ears. A sound to the right of us reaches the right ear perhaps .0001 second before it reaches the left. This tiny time lag is unconsciously perceived and allows us to localize the object in the direction of the ear stimulated first. If you turn your head until the sound strikes both ears at once, the source is directly ahead. Primitives, to pinpoint the source of a sound, slowly shake the head back and forth. Try it sometime when you hear the distant approach of a car.

The sound you hear most often and with greatest interest is the sound of your own voice. You hear it not only through air vibrations which strike your eardrums but through vibrations transmitted directly to the inner ear through your skull. When you chew on a stalk of celery, the loud crunching noise comes mainly through bone conduction. Such bone conduction explains why we hardly recognize a recording of our speech. Many of the low-frequency tones which seem to us to give our voices resonance and power are conducted to our ears through the skull; in a recording they are missing, and so our voices often strike us as thin and weak.

Perhaps hearing will atrophy in a civilization where, increasingly, too much is going on. As a result of this overload, we learn to ignore most of the sound around us, and miss much that could give us pleasure and information. Too bad—because there is a wisdom in hearing which we need.

communiquote 2

Judy L. Haynes

Instructions on how to solve a communiquote are given on page 29. The word list for this puzzle is on page 136; the solution is on page 140. Can you solve it without peeking?

DEFINITIONS

Make aimless marks on paper

$\overline{19}$ $\overline{9}$ $\overline{32}$ $\overline{45}$ $\overline{49}$ $\overline{44}$

Rug cleaning machine

$\overline{36}$ $\overline{27}$ $\overline{11}$ $\overline{3}$ $\overline{33}$ $\overline{48}$

Throw out for nonpayment of rent

$\overline{57}$ $\overline{14}$ $\overline{39}$ $\overline{26}$ $\overline{10}$

Motel sign

$\overline{6}$ $\overline{20}$ $\overline{43}$ $\overline{35}$ $\overline{23}$ $\overline{11}$ $\overline{31}$

Not drunk

$\overline{38}$ $\overline{50}$ $\overline{24}$ $\overline{41}$ $\overline{16}$

Sat. morning TV fare

$\overline{43}$ $\overline{5}$ $\overline{51}$ $\overline{17}$ $\overline{54}$ $\overline{2}$ $\overline{8}$

Remove whiskers

$\overline{29}$ $\overline{46}$ $\overline{22}$ $\overline{36}$ $\overline{18}$

The Rockies

$\overline{53}$ $\overline{12}$ $\overline{28}$ $\overline{23}$ $\overline{10}$ $\overline{27}$ $\overline{47}$ $\overline{13}$ $\overline{29}$

Newspaper eye-catcher

$\overline{34}$ $\overline{15}$ $\overline{20}$ $\overline{52}$ $\overline{56}$ $\overline{39}$ $\overline{42}$ $\overline{37}$

On an annual basis

$\overline{1}$ $\overline{25}$ $\overline{5}$ $\overline{55}$ $\overline{40}$ $\overline{31}$

Tippecanoe's partner

$\overline{17}$ $\overline{58}$ $\overline{40}$ $\overline{30}$ $\overline{51}$

Better than a triple (baseball)

$\overline{4}$ $\overline{54}$ $\overline{21}$ $\overline{7}$ $\overline{16}$ $\overline{3}$ $\overline{42}$

SOLUTION

$\overline{1}$ $\overline{2}$ $\overline{3}$ $\overline{4}$ $\overline{5}$ $\overline{6}$ $\overline{7}$ $\overline{8}$ $\overline{9}$ $\overline{10}$

$\overline{11}$ $\overline{12}$ $\overline{13}$ $\overline{14}$ $\overline{15}$ $\overline{16}$ $\overline{17}$ $\overline{18}$ $\overline{19}$ $\overline{20}$ $\overline{21}$ $\overline{22}$ $\overline{23}$

$\overline{24}$ $\overline{25}$ $\overline{26}$ $\overline{27}$ $\overline{28}$ $\overline{29}$ $\overline{30}$ $\overline{31}$ $\overline{32}$ $\overline{33}$ $\overline{34}$ $\overline{35}$ $\overline{36}$ $\overline{37}$

$\overline{38}$ $\overline{39}$ $\overline{40}$ $\overline{41}$ $\overline{42}$ $\overline{43}$ $\overline{44}$ $\overline{45}$ $\overline{46}$ $\overline{47}$ $\overline{48}$.

$\overline{49}$ $\overline{50}$ $\overline{51}$ $\overline{52}$ $\overline{53}$ $\overline{54}$ $\overline{55}$ $\overline{56}$ $\overline{57}$ $\overline{58}$

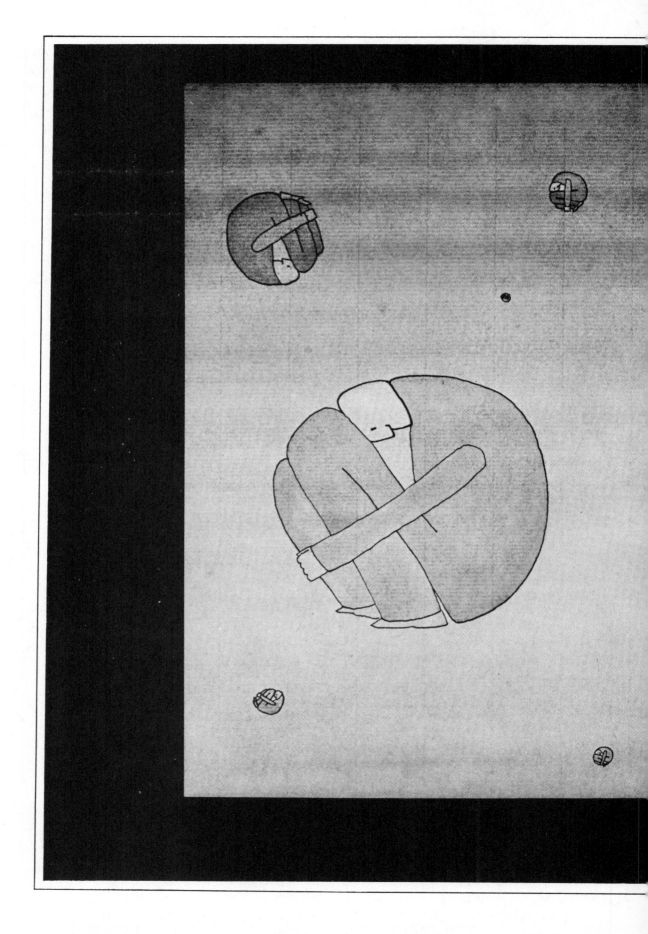

Reach out for someone.
To communicate is the beginning of understanding. AT&T

a snob's guide to tv

Larry Tritten

Reliable polls designed to investigate the viewing habits of the television-watching public have produced conclusive evidence that every major TV show has its unique and specific audience. Moreover, the average viewer of a given program reflects, to a large extent, the values of that program. The polls have shown, for example, that most of the viewers of the lately departed *Hee Haw* were located in rural areas and that in New York City, the show often failed to attract even ten percent of the people watching television during its time slot. Consequently, if you are the regular viewer of a program to whose audience you do not properly belong—if you are, say, a distinguished philosophy professor at Columbia who can't start your day without watching *Captain Kangaroo*—then you are helping to louse up the reliability of the polls. To prevent this, we offer the following convenient guide, which illustrates just who and what you should be in order to watch the following programs.

HOW TO WATCH GUNSMOKE

Whittle. At parties, ask the host where he keeps his spittoon. Be suspicious of any guy who orders a mixed drink and always call homosexuals "goddamn pansies." Get wind-burned. Stand around tight-lipped, with your hands thrust into your hip pockets, and squint into the sunlight. Shave with a straight razor, even though you cut yourself a lot. Be laconic. Sweat. Draw to an inside straight once in a while, just for the hell of it. Bank at Wells Fargo. Carry a bowie knife and a honing block. Punch people hard on the arm to show how much you like them. Be able to smoke without using your hands, drink your coffee black and always order a steak by saying, "Burn one for me." Know what fetlocks and withers are and refer to your girlfriend as "my little filly." Whistle Merle Haggard songs while you commute to work in the city in a pickup truck—and remember that Roy Rogers was once a member of the Sons of the Pioneers. Be pissed off about the firing of General MacArthur. Wonder whatever happened to Lash LaRue. Talk about "the winter of '48"—or whenever the last "really big" winter was. Ignore pop tabs on beer cans and insist on using your "church key." OK comment: "Yup." OK bumper-sticker: *Calgary Stampede.*

HOW TO WATCH THE SECRET STORM

Be an unmarried female of indeterminate age and sex. Wear your high school class ring. Cry at weddings. Cry at funerals. Cry at traffic jams. Chew gum to stretch your coffee breaks. Chew your fingernails. Own all of Rod McKuen's books and Glenn Yarbrough's records. Think of Shakey's Pizza Parlor as an Italian restaurant. Lunch at Woolworth's. While out walking, always worry about being sexually assaulted—and be disappointed when you're not. Read your horoscope religiously—in the daily newspaper and in *Cosmopolitan*. Date a data-processing-school dropout who brings you Whitman Samplers, then read *Better Homes & Gardens* to see what you can make out of the empty boxes. Think of Seven and Seven as a cocktail. When you pick up *Time*, turn to the "Medicine" section first. Be concerned about what's happening to Jackie Onassis. Have a racy friend who keeps the light on during sexual relations. Wear curlers to the Ice Follies. On your birthday, get drunk alone, cry, walk around the house naked, talk dirty and smoke a Tiparillo. OK heroines: Dr. Joyce Brothers, Peg Bracken, Abigail Van Buren. OK question: "But are you sure you'll respect me afterward?"

HOW TO WATCH AMERICAN BANDSTAND

Be a card-carrying WASP teenager from the suburbs and drive your own Camaro to prove it. Argue with your friends about whether Bobby Sherman is heavier than Davy Jones. Never wonder if Dick Clark is Dorian Gray, because you don't know who Dorian Gray is. Carry a picture of Grand Funk Railroad in your wallet. Never smoke pot, but brag to your friends about the dynamite someone turned you on to last week. Fondly remember great golden oldies like *Louie, Louie* and *Mrs. Brown, You've Got a Lovely Daughter*. Smear yourself with Clearasil twice a day, even though you've never had a pimple. Think Paul is still cute, but wonder if poor John has gone crazy. Envy everyone who appears on *Bandstand*. Subscribe to *Hit Parader* and think of *Rolling Stone* as a magazine for old people. Know the names of the whole Partridge family. If you're a girl, worry about your nipples' showing when you go without a bra. If you're a boy, be able to spot a girl without a bra at 20 feet. OK comment: "It's got a good beat, but I didn't like the lyrics, so I gave it a sixty-three." OK poster: *The Archies Live!*

HOW TO WATCH THE DORIS DAY SHOW

Be a 40-year-old virgin who's been married twice. Have a dangerous amount of cheery energy and be alarmingly healthy. Drive a Valiant and tape a plastic daisy to the tip of its radio antenna. Laugh at Freudian slips and blush when you see pictures of the Washington Monument. Be a den mother. Snap your fingers to Muzak. Never pet on the first date and during a goodnight kiss, remember to keep your legs crossed. Think of Erich

Segal as an intellectual. Have a cat named Mr. Whiskers and be undecided about whether or not you should have him "fixed." Recall when *Family Circle* was seven cents, but still think of it as a terrific bargain at 25. Be embarrassed about dirty dreams in which you and Johnny Carson play croquet. Propose a game of charades at a New Year's Eve party and, if that fails, perform all your old college cheers. Go skiing on weekends and spend all your time skiing. Keep a sex manual under your mattress. Always be on a diet, always eat like a wolf and always have a perfect figure. OK risque comment: "Excuse me, I've got to go to the little-girls' room."

HOW TO WATCH MISSION: IMPOSSIBLE

Keep up to date on Balkan politics. Wear wash-and-wear bulletproof suits. Amuse yourself by doing the crossword puzzle in *Pravda* and by building a small Moog synthesizer in your spare time—constructing it entirely of beer cans and old portable radios. Be able to disguise yourself as Mao Tse-tung, Pierre Trudeau, Kwame Nkrumah and Golda Meir, all at once. Have an affair with the sultry daughter of a democratic South American premier who was tragically assassinated in a rightwing military coup—and always search her for concealed weapons before making love. Be a regular at an Albanian restaurant and always pay in leks. Own a Rolex watch that tells the time in any two world zones, the date, the temperature, how far away lightning struck, the latest diamond-market quotations and where tyranny will strike next—and that also functions as a camera and a tachometer. If anything goes wrong with it, fix it yourself. Dabble in hypnotism, *kung fu* and brain surgery. Have an account in a Swiss bank and tell your number to everybody. Talk fondly about the last time you were in Botswana. Smoke only Balkan Sobranies, even though you prefer cherry-flavored Roi-Tans. Suspect all friends and relatives of being subversives and occasionally tail them for a few days—and just to be safe, tail yourself once in a while. Sometimes wear a monocle. Make nostalgic comments about the decline of the Orient Express. OK comment: "There'll never be another Ian Fleming."

HOW TO WATCH ORAL ROBERTS

Complain that Billy Graham is too liberal. Tear the underwear section out of the Sears catalog so your kids won't be exposed to hard-core pornography. Have a white-Angora cross hanging from your car's rearview mirror. Think of the wedding of a Methodist and a Presbyterian as a mixed marriage. Pray every night for peace, right after you pray that we bomb North Vietnam back into the Stone Age. Believe that all massage parlors are actually fronts for houses of prostitution. Have a complete collection of *Reader's Digest Condensed Books* that you've never read. Feel that your Thursday nights are empty now that Jim Nabors has been canceled. Keep a collection of French postcards out in the chicken shed. Put your hands on the TV during the faith-healing prayer and feel better afterward. Don't smoke, drink, play cards, swear or dance—and do as little breathing as possible. Avoid close contact with the opposite sex (sexual relations with your legal mate are permissible as long as rubber gloves and surgical masks are worn and you don't enjoy yourself). OK heroes: Pat Boone, Billy James Hargis. OK comment: "I think George Wallace is going soft." OK bumper sticker: *Hit Me! I'm Going To Heaven Anyway!*

HOW TO WATCH MARCUS WELBY, M.D.

Browse in pharmacies. Buy everything that the ads tell you three out of four doctors recommend. Jog. Do isometric exercises and drive a late-model ambulance. Send your friends medicine balls for Christmas. Wear orthopedic shoes. If you're a girl, wear support hose. Subscribe to the *Journal of Abdominal Surgery* and *Cancer News*, and flaunt words like frontoparietal and caduceus. At the drop of a forceps, be able to tell at least 300 gruesomely detailed stories about operations. Smoke nontobacco cigarettes in a tar-eliminating holder

and quit smoking once a week. Always carry a thermometer, plenty of Band-Aids, some splints and an airsickness bag—and when you visit the zoo, take along a snakebite kit. Whenever a friend complains of a slight headache, mention Rocky Mountain spotted fever, malaria, yaws and cholera. Be torn between visiting the Mayo Clinic and Forest Lawn on your vacation. Whenever you fill out a form that asks for the name of your doctor, attach a separate sheet listing your general practitioner, opthamologist, dermatologist, podiatrist, proctologist, dentist, chiropractor and veterinarian. Boil all the water you drink and sleep under a mosquito net. Gargle with Listerine but think it tastes great. Have your last words carefully prepared. Be on the verge of leaving your body to science. OK question: "What's your favorite sickness?" OK hobby: revising your will.

HOW TO WATCH SESAME STREET

Be a bright, attentive, prepubescent child or a thin, handsome, 40ish divorced female psychologist who has written a book about lactation and who has a daughter majoring in education at Brandeis, a fixed smile and an impotent lover.

HOW TO WATCH THE SIX O'CLOCK NEWS

Have a good stiff shot of bourbon.

ANSWERS FOR COMMUNICODE 2

Eulogy	Lecture
Sales Pitch	Sermon
Inaugural Address	Persuasive Speech
Announcement	Farewell Speech
Oration	After-Dinner Speech

This article gives examples of the way some top executives use extrasensory perception (ESP) to make decisions. The same techniques can work in everyday life.

HOW SUCCESSFUL MEN MARK DECISIONS

Edythe Cudlipp

You are hunting for a parking space and have to make a decision. Should you continue down the street you are on, or turn left even though you have already been down that street and found nothing? "Something" tells you to turn left. You do, and find a car just pulling out.

This is an example of a simple, everyday decision, one that is reached by weighing the evidence and then following a hunch, that compulsive "sixth" sense that is also called extrasensory perception, or ESP.

How about a more complicated decision? Take the business executive in charge of an electronics firm. Business is good; the company is making money. Should he use the profits to expand the output of the firm, or should he stand pat on the basis that business may have reached its saturation point? He feeds all the available data into a computer, which is programmed to project future business. While it says to stand pat, the executive decides instead to expand—not on logic but because he *feels* business is going to get even better. Only time will tell if his decision is the right one, but time has proven him right before.

In other words, although computers are being programmed to do just about everything that man can do (and do it faster and more accurately in some cases), we can all take comfort in the knowledge that only man can make the decisions that really count. At the Newark College of Engineering in Newark, N.J., Professor John Mihalasky is conducting experiments on how top executives make decisions. His research shows that the higher an executive climbs on the ladder of success, the better he is in using intuitive judgment, or ESP.

Professor Mihalasky, who has degrees in both management and engineering, defines ESP as an awareness of, or a response to, an external event or influence, not apprehended by presently known sensory means. Precognition, the phase of ESP with which he is directly concerned, is the obtaining of information to do with the future.

This is the kind of information that no computer can really be programmed for. One example is the executive in a large department store who is charged with buying fashions. A few years ago, the buyer who bought maxi-coats because they were new couldn't sell them. On the other hand, the buyer who felt this was the year for maxis, even though they were a failure last year, has had his decision justified. Then, there is the automobile executive who "feels" that one design has "something" that's going to appeal to people, even though all three designs from which he has to decide are equally safe. A real-estate developer who has to buy land for a new development may select property farther out from the city than his assistants think wise, yet every lot sells as soon as it goes on the market. When he's asked why he chose that land, he says, "I just knew it was right."

None of these people really had "inside" information. They weighed the evidence and made a decision about the future. Since information of the future is the basic ingredient in making so many decisions, the first step in the professor's research was to evolve a test dealing with the future. The "future test" is basically a guessing game. Using computer cards, the person is asked to guess at a 100 digit number, with each digit being a number between 0 and 9. For example, 987.

Actually, the person is guessing at a number that has not yet been determined at the time of the test. The number is still in the future. Later a computer generates the number, and that number is compared with the guess for a real test of future information. The reason for using the computer is to avoid personal bias—not touched by human hands—and for speed in obtaining results.

The big question was whether the test had any validity. That is, was there a relationship between how a man does on the test, how he does on his job? From among hundreds of executives, they culled out those who were chief executives, who had been on their jobs at least five years, and who actually made decisions. Then, they looked at the profit records of the companies the executives headed, on the theory that an executive's decisions would be reflected in the company's profit or loss record.

The chances of guessing the number purely by chance are about five to eight times in a thousand guesses, according to Mihalasky's experiments. Those decision-making executives who had increased their companies' profits by 100 per cent scored way above chance, as high as about 12 per cent, or 12 times in a thousand.

Another part of the test was to determine what types of personalities might be likely to have precognitive ability. For this, they used the two-part multiple-choice test on to distinguish between dynamic and nondynamic personalities.

Professor Mihalasky explains, "While we don't want to get trapped into the semantics of what's dynamic and what isn't, by dynamic we mean the person who is always in a rush: This is the 'time is money, I've got to do it today, and I can't wait until tomorrow' individual. The nondynamic person is the one who says, 'So what if it doesn't get done today? It will get done tomorrow.' We found that a person's attitude towards time equates with his precognitive ability. In general, the person always in a rush, the dynamic person, tends to be a better guesser than the one to whom time means nothing."

He adds, "We are also interested in learning whether the executives believe in ESP, and what relationship belief has to decision-making." Many executives told Professor Mihalasky that, in making a decision, they often reach a point where, in spite of all the data at their fingertips, they can't accept what the data is telling them. Or the data may be too insignificant or unreliable, yet still they have to make a decision. They may not admit to using ESP, or believing in it, but they'll say, "I had a feeling," or "I thought that if..."

Many of the books that have been written about logical decision-making bear this out. Experts in management whom the professor has talked to, or whose books he has read, will go on and on about relying on data. Yet they finally admit that there is such a thing as illogical or emotional decision-making. This, he says, is what people do most of the time. Furthermore, experts admit that there are some people who have this ability to an uncanny degree. The question is how to spot them.

Professor Mihalasky points out, "What has happened in the past is that you have had to spot these people by seeing the results. Then, you pushed them along.

"We think that now we have a tool, in these tests, to identify such people early, ahead of the time when they have to make the do-or-die decisions. We feel that we're ready to go out in the field and say, 'Mr. Chairman of the Board, you're considering five men for president. You've given them all sorts of psychological tests for facts and attitudes. In addition, how about giving them this test for precognition?"

At the same time, he admits that one problem with ESP is that people think it's not scientific. "You've got to convince people that it is not *nonscientific*. The fact that you don't know how it works, or where it comes from, doesn't mean that it doesn't exist and so you can't use it.

"This is not a phenomenon that's metaphysical or mystical. We definitely feel that we are dealing with a physical phenomenon, and we've got to learn more about this energy form. For instance, scientists have always thought that nothing could be faster than the speed of light. Now physicists think that there *are* particles that *do* travel faster. I think—and hope—that the same thing will happen with ESP once science makes a thorough investigation."

Like many psychologists and others who have worked with ESP, Professor Mihalasky believes that everybody has it to some degree. Everybody gets hunches or "feelings" at one time. They can even be reflected in our attitudes towards people.

Personnel people tell him that many times they know the minute someone walks in the door whether the person will be hired or not. While not hiring a person is no indication of their success in making the right decision, the results of their judgment in hiring a certain person often bear them out.

Once a person gets a hunch, of course, he has to have the courage to follow it up. Because of this, intelligence has nothing to do with ESP and may even be a handicap, "since precognition is a nonlogical

process. You don't have to be smart to be a good guesser.

"Often, the more intelligent a person is, the more logical he is, and there is less chance that he has allowed precognitive ability to develop, even though it is an unconscious process. Children, for example, are more precognitive than adults are.

"To develop precognitive ability, you have to allow it to come out. The more you allow it to appear, the more you make use of it, the more it happens. In this respect, we read constantly about the executives and others who sleep with pads and pencils next to their beds. Well, one way to get precognitive information is through dreams."

Not only is precognition unconscious, it also works after a three-Martini lunch. The professor gave a test to a group of executives at a convention dinner, after everyone had taken liberal advantage of the free drinks. Those executives who tested out as dynamic, and fulfilled the other criteria, still scored better than the nondynamics.

None of this means that Professor Mihalasky is advocating throwing computers out the window. They have their places, and he does utilize them in his testing. Too many people, however, have let computers push the aspect of logical decision-making too far. He points out, "I think that there is an area where computers serve a useful purpose, especially at the lower levels of decision-making and management. There, the chances are pretty good that data is more reliable, more valid. This is a narrow area, nevertheless, and it doesn't deal with the future.

"The further up the ladder a person goes, the more he is dealing with the future. Data becomes less available and less reliable. There is less experience to fall back on. The

person has to go by his own personal intuition or precognition.

"At the moment," he continues, "people have become data addicts. They think that the computer is the salvation of the world, whereas actually computers are only idiot machines that people program.

ARE YOU A GOOD DECISION-MAKER?

In each of the two groups below, pick the statement that best describes how you feel. Then look at the analysis to find out if you have the qualities to be a good decision maker.

ATTITUDE TO TIME: Of the five metaphors below, indicate the one you like best:
1. A dashing waterfall
2. A galloping horseman
3. An old woman spinning
4. A vast expanse of sky
5. A quiet motionless ocean

ATTITUDE TO ESP: Do you think some people are sometimes able to obtain information by ESP?
1. Sure about it
2. This is a possibility
3. It might be so or not
4. It seems unlikely
5. It is impossible.

If your attitude toward time is either 1 or 2, you're dynamic. If you selected 4 or 5, you're nondynamic. Statement 3 in both groups is neutral. As far as belief in ESP goes, the people who are best at making decisions are non-believing dynamists, and the next best are dynamists who believe in ESP. Even if the test seems simple, Professor Mihalasky, claims that his experiments prove that its's accurate.

This always happens with a new item. Eventually, the computer will take its rightful place in the full spectrum of tools available to man."

While Professor Mihalasky's experiments are aimed at decision-making in business, what he has learned can be used by everybody. Every one of us, every day of his life, is faced with making decisions. Sometimes the decisions may be simple ones, such as the best and quickest way to get home from work at night. Sometimes they may affect our lives, like a decision to change jobs.

It may pay you to wait for that "feeling," to expect that precognitive voice out of the blue, and to pursue it. The difficulty is that once the decision is made, you can't always be sure whether you were right.

If you're driving down the highway and "something" tells you to take another road, you have to make a decision. If you continue on, you may find a traffic jam, proving that your precognition was right. Once you turn off, you'll never know whether the hunch was right or wrong—but you will have the satisfaction of knowing that, like many executives you made a decision.

<table>
<tr><td colspan="2">WORD LIST FOR COMMUNIQUOTE 2</td></tr>
<tr><td>Cartoon</td><td>Homerun</td></tr>
<tr><td>Sober</td><td>Tyler</td></tr>
<tr><td>Vacancy</td><td>Yearly</td></tr>
<tr><td>Evict</td><td>Headline</td></tr>
<tr><td>Vacuum</td><td>Mountains</td></tr>
<tr><td>Doodle</td><td>Shave</td></tr>
</table>

how to cope with social disasters

Barbara Walters

Barbara Watters (of the Today TV show) discusses her experiences in coping with "Foot in the Mouth" incidents. Her examples are primarily from cocktail party settings, but the suggestions she makes can apply to other situations as well.

Disaster is when you have arrived at a late-afternoon wedding, wearing your bright-red double-knit, to find all the other guests in long gowns and dinner jackets.

Disaster is when you have picked up a charming ornament and asked the hostess where it came from. She answers, "It was my great-grandmother's," with which you drop it, and it smashes to bits.

Disaster is also when you have informed a group of people that you met Mr. and Mrs. Smithright last night and Mrs. Smithright is a knockout. And a chunky frump says, "That's odd. I'm Mrs. Smithright, and I was at home last night."

You can pretend to faint, but this is a temporary measure. You've got to do better than that, and you get marks for quickness. In the first case, I would tell the bride's mother, once, that you had to attend another affair and couldn't find time to change without missing the ceremony, which you couldn't bear to do. In the second situation, you apologize to the hostess, who will appreciate how bad you feel, and then you prowl the shops the next day until you find something beautiful. Send it to her, with a note that you know it won't make up the loss, but you hope she'll enjoy it.

Tell Mrs. Smithright that you must have met another Smithright—is her husband twenty-six, bearded, and on crutches from an automobile accident? No? Well, it was someone else entirely, then. But if you've identified him irretrievably, look adorably addled as you remember that the knockout was married to someone else, who

soon dragged her off. It probably won't be believed, but it saves Mrs. Smithright's pride.

Some people are social-disaster-prone, as some people have a proclivity for getting into bone-breaking accidents. They're the kind who, when talking to a grotesquely fat person, find words like "diet" and "overweight" and "blubber" popping into their sentences. Subliminal malice? Maybe.

Shy people suffer another kind of disaster. When they're set down among people they don't know well, their confidence collapses, and they see themselves as the only people in the room lacking wit and grace. Despair sweeps over them, numbing reflexes. They stumble into people sipping hot coffee and forget the name of their best freind.

Unhappily, most of us have experienced both kinds of disaster. We've all spoken too hastily and tasted our own shoe leather, and we've all felt hopelessly inept.

Sometimes the result is so paralyzing that it's impossible to function for the moment. Maybe you'll be lucky, and someone with the golden gift of tact will be on the scene. There is a famous illustration of this—the perfect hostess who, when a guest was mortified after knocking over his wineglass, waited for a few minutes and then upset her own.

Marion Javits, wife of the Senator, saved an embarrassing situation for Johnny Carson at a dinner party we all attended. They were seated beside each other, and Johnny, a surprisingly shy and uneasy man in private life, spilled his soup during the first course and later dripped some gravy on his tie. Instead of ignoring it, which wouldn't have improved Johnny's discomfiture much, or being solicitous, which would have made him feel worse, Marion made a joke of it all, and Johnny joined in until they were kidding each other.

When something is spilled or broken, the offender is aghast. There's a trace of the child's fear of punishment in his reaction, and a good deal of shame, and anger against himself. It is the obligation of the hostess, *promptly,* to make the person feel as comfortable as possible. Make the broken object seem less important. One heroine cried, "Thank heavens that horror is finally broken. I've hated it for years!" Make the cleanup quick and casual, and pick up the conversation where it was interrupted.

If you're the offender and you've broken something that can be replaced, do so as soon as possible. If something has been stained in a spill, perhaps you can have your cleaner pick it up the next day. If these measures aren't feasible, send flowers or a gift, and a note of apology.

Another kind of disaster is the faux pas, and I've committed some beauts right in front of the millions who watch the Today show. Not long ago, a guest referred to Albert Schweitzer, and I asked brightly how old Dr. Schweitzer was. The guest looked at me in amazement and said, "But he's dead." As I prayed for an immediate power failure, that old wheeze "I didn't even know he was sick" flashed across my mind, but I knew I had to resign myself to the egg on my face. I confessed frankly, "I'm so embarrassed, how stupid of me. Of course I should have remembered he died some time ago." And then I asked my next question.

I expected that there would be a landslide of derisive mail, but there wasn't a single letter about my blooper. I think most viewers were sympathetic, maybe having blundered that way themselves once or twice, and perhaps they appreciated my honesty.

The point I want to make is: Don't try to bluff your way out unless, as with Mrs. Smithright, someone else's feelings are involved. Admit right away that you made a mistake. You can't lose any more ground than you already have, and you might pick up a little—the ability to say, "I was wrong" is exceedingly rare these days and merits respect.

You can cut down the risk of an awkward situation by not asking about an absent spouse unless you know the person rather well. "We're getting a divorce" is a hard act to follow. If it does happen that some remark of yours obliges the other person to explain that his marriage is breaking up, don't say that you're sorry—

presumably, he's glad. Say, "Forgive me, I didn't know," and change the subject.

A woman I know was upset for days after making this kind of error. She had just been introduced to a couple, Bill and Nancy, and she couldn't wait to tell Nancy that they had a friend in common, Nancy's former roommate. Nancy looked bewildered for a moment and then explained, "I'm afraid you must be thinking of my husband's *first* wife. She's also named Nancy."

My friend had the aplomb to say, "Well, that's my faux pas for the night," and quickly asked Bill and Nancy where they were living and if they liked it.

This kind of slip is easily understood, but many come close to being unforgivable. One woman at a dinner party sneered that some task was so simple "even a mongolian idiot could do it," and later learned that two guests were the parents of a mongoloid baby. It's best, of course, never to joke about defects. Jerry Lewis' mock-spastic act horrifies me, though I know he is a kind man and a pillar of the muscular-dystrophy fund. I wish he wouldn't exploit an affliction to get a laugh.

If you have made such a ghastly blunder, apologize. Tell the people affected that you've learned a lesson, and undoubtedly you have. They'll understand your agony: sometimes very deep friendships begin from such a calamity.

Then there's the time you remark, "I've just read the worst junk you ever saw, Fred Fuller's column"—and a stranger in the group says, "I'm Fred Fuller. Which column do you mean?" When you get your voice back, tell him he's allowed one punch, or tell him you're celebrated statewide for your lack of literary taste, or tell him you'd be glad to get him a drink, because you're on your way to the bar to order arsenic for yourself.

A sweet man I met at a reception told me he watched the Today show every morning and had observed the progress of my pregnancy with pleasure as I grew rounder and rounder every passing day until I announced the birth of our baby. Friends of mine who were present became acutely uncomfortable, knowing that our daughter is adopted; but I didn't take offense at all. I realized that the man was only trying to express interest and would feel terrible when he learned about his error. I was worried about him.

It's a fact that it is much more comfortable to be in a position of the person who has been offended than to be the unfortunate cause of it. Victims have a moment of hurt, and they can display generosity and sweet forgiveness, while the offender is all but destroyed. I notice that people at fault in a situation usually need warmth and support more desperately than the injured one.

If you've made a social blunder, confess and apologize, hoping for graciousness, and then *shut up.* Don't spend the rest of the night describing what you did, trying to wear out the guilt of it by public contrition. Live with your mistake in silence; you'll recover eventually and perhaps be the better for it.

It used to be a major disaster to arrive at a formal party dressed informally, or the other way around; but today almost anything goes anywhere. Hats rarely are obligatory for women, even at funerals and weddings, and only small towns still honor the spanking-white kid gloves as the hallmark of a real lady. Most social events draw such a conglomerate of minis, midis, maxis, and pant suits that you can probably wear a nightgown and go unnoticed.

Curiously, it now is the men who worry about being dressed appropriately. They dread wearing the only three-piece suit amid the cardigans, or a turtleneck surrounded by ties. At some events, fringed buckskin and gray flannel rub shoulders with mutual unconcern, but in general, most men like the anonymity of dressing like every other man in the room.

I listened to my friend Constance Hope, a top New York public-relations consultant and a superb hostess, save the situation for a guest who arrived at her dinner party in a black tie, the only man in formal dress. As Constance greeted him and noticed his embarrassment, she squeezed his arm and murmured, "Good for you. I told everyone that it was black tie, but they all forgot. You're the only one who got it right."

If you can't handle how awkward you feel about the way you're dressed, tell the hostess that you have another affair to attend (which will explain your attire), and leave early.

Sickness can be another kind of social disaster. I'll never forget the anniversary party my husband and I gave a few years ago, when New York was having a flu epidemic. All during the day of the party, I was kept busy answering the telephone as wives called to say their husbands were sick and couldn't make it, or husbands phoned to say their wives had the flu. As the party kept shrinking, I removed place settings and juggled the place cards.

The survivors gathered at the dinner table, but in the middle of the soup course, NBC Radio's Ben Grauer left the table. I took his temperature, which was 103. After that, other guests began to fold, some of them stretching out on the beds and some on couches. We had invited twenty people, but only eleven finished dinner. I began to feel we were doing a scene from a bad murder mystery.

The role of the hostess in such a crisis is, obviously, to care for her ailing guests. You offer a quiet bedroom, where the guest can lie down for a while. If the sickness is beyond the headache class and he thinks he'd better leave, make certain that transportation is available and that he needs no further help. The next morning, telephone to inquire how he's feeling.

But it is also the responsibility of the ailing guest to cause the minimum of fuss. If you can summon up the stamina, say nothing, and stay at the party for a civil length of time. If you're feeling too wretched to last, make your explanation to the hostess inconspicuously, and leave without a roll-call farewell of the other guests. Send a note the next day expressing your regret at having to leave such a great party.

If you feel ill before the party starts, call the hostess and tell her, "*We* won't be able to come." Don't say, "I can't make it," or, "George is sick and can't come to your party," because both dangle the suggestion that the healthy person is hoping to go alone. Let the hostess ask you to come by yourself, if that suits her table arrangement or the kind of gathering she has arranged. She is in the best position to decide if a single will fit in or not.

Another possible upset is the social argument. But I often think that we worry too much about dissension. I lean to the view that a good clash can be splendid, for the participants and for the audience. On the Today program we often go out of our way to arrange confrontation. For instance, when the very liberal Dr. Benjamin Spock came to the show to publicize his book *Decent and Indecent,* it was no accident that we also invited the very conservative William Buckley.

When two people are squaring off for an argument, don't feel reflexively that you must stop it at all costs. Size it up. The main consideration, as in the tumbling fights of small boys, is whether someone is likely to be hurt. If the opponents are a good match intellectually, let them go to it. Don't participate, and don't defend them apologetically; they're big boys.

If you're the one drawn into the argument, make the same evaluation. Can you hold your own? Can the other person? It is only when people feel overmatched, or start to lose, that emotions get out of control.

If the argument deteriorates and becomes personal and vicious, end it at once. "Hey, folks," you say in your friendly but strict schoolmarm tone, "this has gone too far. You're making the rest of us uncomfortable, so let's table this discussion."

Almost a worse disaster is the group that can't talk at all. There's an anxious silence suffocating the room. People fidget and stare into their drinks. Someone timidly says that the weather has been awful, and there's a round of "Hasn't it, though," and, "You said it," and, "Just awful," followed by a long, wretched pause, into which someone finally says, "I was in Tulsa last week, and the weather was awful there, too." The observation sinks into the silence, and people go back to listening to their ice cubes melt.

The best hope for rescue is an anecdotal question. It will cheer people up to have something happening at last and give them time to whip up their confidence and enthusiasm. Tell them a statement you heard on television about some topical matter, and ask if everyone agrees with it. Quote from something you've read about education or automation or violence, and ask someone's opinion. Use your family if it can lead to a general discussion—for example: "My teenager came home today and wanted to know if I was a virgin before I was married. How do you think that should be answered?" I'd love to know myself.

SOLUTION FOR COMMUNIQUOTE 2

You have not converted a man because you have silenced him.

Lord Morley

The fable of the 5 blind men and the elephant goes something like this: in order to form an impression of an elephant, each man felt the beast. Unfortunately, each felt a different part and thus had a different (and erroneous) mental image of an elephant. When they discussed their impressions, you can imagine the confusion.

Here are 3 endings to the fable. You can pick the one you like, and live happily ever after.

The Blind Men and the Elephant:
Three Ends to One Tale

Raymond J. Corsini

Many centuries have passed after the fact, but is it possible to discover the end of the tale of the Blind Men and the Elephant? Ali thought the Elephant to be like a spear, Bul like a fan, Con like a wall, Dor like a tree stump, and Eri like a rope. What happened thereafter has not been told. It is possible that man's fate depends on the end of the tale. Three endings are given below: the reader may take his choice.

END ONE

Ali, the. . .eldest, spake: "I am the eldest, and consequently the wisest. I am also the first to have felt the Elephant and now the first to speak about him. Moreover, I felt him carefully, to the very end. He ends in a sharp point. He is hard, long, and smooth, and is like a spear which curves gently. My description of the Elephant may be regarded as definitive."

Bul spoke next: "It is true, Ali, that you are aged. Hence your faculties are dim. Also, if you are right, then I must be wrong. This is impossible, since phenomenologically reality is as I see it. Far from being like a spear, the Elephant is soft, wide, flat, and pulpy—very much like a fan."

"Reality is reality," stated Con. "I kicked the Elephant. He is massive, like a wall. He is limitless, infinite. I could find no end. Oh, the poverty of philosophy, the smallness of men who reduce infinity to the proportions of their own mean perceptions!"

Dor began to whirl his staff about his head, screaming: "No, no, no. Wrong, wrong, wrong! I started with fundamentals, from the ground up. The Elephant is like the trunk of a tree. By Allah and Moreno, you are all wrong."

At this point, his mouth frothing, Eri began to lay about him. "Liars, Adlerians, Catholics, Negroes..."

Then the others began to labor each other with *their* heavy, iron-shafted staffs, yelling meanwhile, "Infidels, Rogerians, Trotskyites, Mormons, Semanticists, Jews, McCarthyites, Collectivists, Syndicalists, Behaviorists, Episcopalians, Dianneticists, Transactionists, Freudolators..."

After a while, all was quiet. And when people came by, they found that all but one of the Blind men were dead. One of the passers-by knelt beside the sole survivor, and seeing the dying man's lips moving, bent close.

"The others, are they dead?"

"Yes."

"Ah, then...then...I am right. The Elephant is like...."But he then expired, and to this day no one knows what the Elephant is like.

END TWO
Seminar-Wise, the Blind Men gathered at a conference table, and Ali, the eldest, spake: "We have long been curious to know exactly what an elephant is like, and we have already gathered enough preliminary data to indicate that each of us has had different perceptions. Since the whole is at least the sum of its parts, let us try to reconstruct the beast by correlating the data we have gathered. From my experiential frame of reference, this is how the Elephant appears to me...."

And so the Blind Men discussed the Elephant at length, and finally they arrived at an integration and summation of their perceptions. Thus they created what might be called the Eclectic Elephant, which was approved by all concerned, and became The Elephant.

The Elephant was concluded to be a creature which had for a head a single spear-shaped protrusion; probably for decoration but perhaps for protection from the sun, it had a kind of shade or parasol or fan; protrusion and fan were mounted on an enormous, wall-like body, upheld by a single stump-like leg; the creature ended with a rope-like tail.

A joint monograph on the Elephant was written by the Blind Men and was published in the *Hindustani Journal of Experimental and Comparative Zoology*. It remains the basic reference on the subject.

END THREE
Ali, the eldest, spake: "It is evident that since we are blind we cannot really know what the Elephant is like." Bul nodded, "We can each get a part of the beast, but the whole escapes us. Our limitations are only too evident. And even a combination of our perceptions..."

"...is inadequate," added Con, "because the whole is more than..."

"There is probably more to the Elephant than what we have felt," stated Dor. "Perhaps if we called in still another blind man to feel the Elephant, he would see it as a volley-ball, a lawn-sprinkler, or an Austin car. We can never hope to understand. We are too mean and limited to obtain a just conception of this vast and noble beast. How may we ever realize this?"

"There is only one way," suggested Eri. "It is evident that what we must do to understand the Elephant is to ask someone who can *see*."

"A higher authority!" the other Blind Men shouted. "That's what we need."

So they went to consult a child of high reputation—the same child who seen the Emperor as he was. "What is the Elephant like?" they asked.

"He is purple, has three heads, sixteen legs, crawls on his belly, and eats with his nose."

"And the spear?"

"It grows from his three eyes and is twelve ells long."

"And the fan?"

"He has hundreds. They flap in the wind."

"And the wall?"

"It extends for miles."

"And the stump?"

"A wart-like decoration."

"And the rope?"

"He hooks it on trees and climbs it."

And so the Blind Men were content.

SELAH

CREDITS

Page 1
Quotation from George Miller, "1969—Where Can We Go from Here?" Reprinted from *Psychology Today* Magazine, December 1969. Copyright © Communications/Research/Machines, Inc.

Page 2
"How Words Change Our Lives," by S. I. Hayakawa, *The Saturday Evening Post,* December 27, 1958, 22 ff. Reprinted by permission of the Saturday Evening Post © 1958, The Curtis Publishing Company, and the author.

Page 5
"Meaning?", by Virginia Bailey, *ETC.,* 27 (1970), 318. Reprinted by permission of the International Society for General Semantics.

"Hot Language and Cool Lives," by Arthur Berger, *ETC.,* 28 (1971), 353-56. Reprinted by permission of the International Society for General Semantics.

Quotations on pages 7 and 102 are from the King James Version of the Bible.

Page 8
"Patterns of Speech," by Max Brandel and Bob Clarke, *Mad* Magazine, April 1973. © 1973 by E. C. Publications, Inc.

Page 11
"Mirror/rorriM" by Loretta Malandro, March 1973, used by permission of the author.

Pages 29, 63, 87, 119, 127
Communiquotes and puzzles by Judy L. Haynes, February 1973, used by permission of the author.

Page 30
"P-A-C at Work," reprinted from Lyman K. Randall, *P-A-C at Work: An-on-the-Job Guide for Answering the Question: "Hey, What's Going on Here?",* pp. 3-29. Copyright © 1971 by American Airlines. Reprinted by permission of the author and American Airlines.

Page 35
"Grin and Bear It" cartoon by George Lichty. Courtesy of Publishers-Hall Syndicate.

Page 36
"Caution! Conversation Being Demolished," by Kaye Starbird, reprinted with permission from the December 1968 Reader's Digest, pp. 107-10. Copyright 1968 by The Reader's Digest Association, Inc. Condensed from the Philadelphia Sunday Bulletin Magazine. Reprinted by permission of Paul R. Reynolds, Inc., 599 Fifth Avenue, New York, N.Y. 10017, and The Reader's Digest Association, Inc.

Page 38
Reprint of advertisement by permission of American Telephone and Telegraph Company, from *Psychology Today,* December 1969.

Pages 40 and 82
"Getting Un-Crossed Up" and "Bed News," by Bernard Gunther, used by permission of the author.

Page 43
"The Short Unhappy Life of the Boy Who Wouldn't Listen," by Joseph Zaitchik, *ETC.,* 18 (1962), 444-48. Reprinted by permission of the International Society for General Semantics.

Page 45
"Semantics and Sexual Communication," by Lester A. Kirkendall, *ETC.,* 23 (1966), 235-44. Reprinted by permission of the International Society for General Semantics. (Footnotes renumbered.)

Page 94
"The Fascinating Funnies," by Fred Dickensen. Reprinted with permission from the November 1971 Reader's Digest. Copyright 1971 by The Reader's Digest Association, Inc. Condensed from *Empire,* October 10, 1971.

Page 96
Wizard of Id cartoon, reprinted by permission of John Hart and Field Enterprises, Inc.

Page 97
Born Loser cartoon, reprinted by permission of Newspaper Enterprise Association.

Page 98
B. C. cartoon, reprinted by permission of John Hart and Field Enterprises, Inc.

Page 99
Doonesbury cartoon, copyright, 1972, G. B. Trudeau/Distributed by Universal Press Syndicate.

Page 100
"Clear Only If Known," by Edgar Dale, *The News Letter* (School of Education, Ohio State University) 31 (April 1966), 1-4. Reprinted by permission of the author.

Page 102
"Here's Music in Your Eyes: Lightshow," by Richard Blystone. Reprinted by permission of The Associated Press.

Page 104
"The Loving Message in a Touch," by Norman M. Lobsenz. Copyright © 1970 by Norman Lobsenz. Reprinted by permission.

Page 106
"Games for Building Warmth and Trust," abridged from *Growth Games,* copyright © 1970, by Howard R. Lewis and Harold R. Streitfeld. Reprinted by permission of Harcourt Brace Jovanovich, Inc.

Page 112
From "Officer Bob Drawing Book" by Fred Hamil. Copyright © 1972 by Chandler Publishing Co. Reprinted from *Focus: Media* by Jess Ritter and Grover Lewis, eds., by permission of the Chandler Publishing Company.

Page 116
"Right You Are if You Say You Are—Obscurely." Reprinted by permission of TIME, The Weekly Newsmagazine; Copyright Time Inc.

Page 120
"Is Language Sexist?", condensed from "One Small Step for Genkind" by Casey Miller and Kate Swift, *The New York Times Magazine,* April 16, 1972. © 1972 by The New York Times Company. Reprinted by permission.

Page 123
"The Tyranny of Women's Liberation," by Corinne Geeting *ETC.,* 28 (September 1971), 357-61. Reprinted by permission of the International Society for General Semantics.

Page 125
"Hearing is a Way of Touching," by John Kord Lagemann. Reprinted with permission from the August 1961 Reader's Digest. Copyright 1969 by The Reader's Digest Association, Inc.

Page 128
Reprint of advertisement by permission of American Telephone and Telegraph Company, from *Psychology Today,* February 1970.

Page 130
"A Snob's Guide to TV," by Larry Tritten, *Playboy,* 18 (October 1971), 137 ff. Reprinted by permission of the author.

DATE DUE

APR 1 1 1980			
NOV 1 9 1982			
MAR 1 1 1983			
APR 9 1985			
MAR 1 4 1986			
MAY 2 2 1987			
JAN 2 2 '88			

DEMCO 38-297